Yellow Cat, Hendry & Me

Dispatches From Life's Front Lines

Bill Brown

Half Hill Press
Dadeville, Alabama

Yellow Cat, Hendry & Me: *Dispatches From Life's Front Lines*

Published by Half Hill Press
Dadeville, Alabama

ISBN: 978-0-9858149-0-8

Library of Congress Control Number: 2012911390

To Adelaide,
my best friend and true North Star,
and to sons Jeff and Jamie,
who have taught me more than I taught them

Contents

Foreword

William Blake Brown and I are not brothers by bloodline, but we claim a special kinship. We're both Southern men, close in age and culture, from middling poor families, and we both went to land-grant colleges, studied journalism, and then set out to seek our fortunes and raise our families. Our paths diverged but never split: Bill stayed in the newsroom while I drifted into the classroom, and eventually we both became managers, Bill a top editor and I an academic clerk.

We met shortly after I'd returned to Auburn, in 1979 while Bill was managing editor of the Columbus Enquirer. One of my older students, who was already working there, sprinkled his conversations with references to an inspiring boss who didn't fit the central-casting model of the hard-drinking, cynical, tough-but tender editor. I took one of my classes over, for a view of real world journalism, but also so that I could meet this fellow.

My student was spot-on right. Bill Brown turned out to be a soft-spoken, even courtly man, who clearly had a habit of listening more than talking and asking questions instead of pontificating. Here, I thought, was a sharp professional who had earned his position, a circumspect editor who knew how to size people up. He impressed me as kindly by nature, not common in editors, and more likely to be amused than indignant.

But the best indicator of his merit was the quality of the newspaper itself. It reflected his news values, his ability to guide but not over direct veteran reporters, to spot talent and recruit it, and to be both a part of his community, and, paradoxically, apart from it— to be as objective as possible but hardly detached or aloof.

When he became executive editor of the Montgomery Advertiser and Alabama Journal, I got to know him better, our wives became friends, and Bill and I conversed by the hour on myriad topics. I came to admire, even envy, his powers of observation and logic, his guts and discipline, and his intellect, which he largely concealed and revealed at the most appropriate occasions.

Bill came by his talent naturally, of course, but he also worked at it, and, as it often follows, had good luck. After graduating from LSU in 1962, he just happened to land a job on one of the best newspapers in the South, the St. Petersburg Times. By age 28, he held one of toughest and most critical of positions in a newsroom, city editor, which requires street smarts, lightning-fast decision making, writing and editing skills, and high-octane energy.

And then after about ten years at The Times, something unusual happened. He up and quit. He and his wife, Adelaide, sold most of their worldly goods, gathered up their two preschool-age sons, went to England, bought a boat, cruised the Thames and the canals of Holland, lived in a chilly flat, fed the boys in their laps and conducted adult conversations with them, and put a definite stamp on their family. Bill calls it a "self-styled sabbatical." It served him well, professionally as well as personally.

Shortly after returning, he was hired by the Tallahassee Democrat as executive city editor, and he quickly caught the eye of the Knight-Ridder bosses. He went to Columbus as managing editor of the Enquirer, then became executive editor of both dailies. His paper won two major national awards for initiating a court case that established the right of the public to be present in state courtrooms for jury selections.

Not surprisingly, Montgomery attracted him. His Louisiana perspective was perfect for the coverage of Alabama politics and society. As managing editor of the morning Advertiser, and soon executive editor of the Advertiser and afternoon Alabama Journal, he directed in-depth reporting on the inner financial doings of the Southern Poverty Law Center, and the Journal won a Pulitzer for a series on the high rate of infant mortality amongst the poor in his circulation area.

During all of this time, I witnessed first hand and through many former students how this subtle, quiet man was a powerful and inspiring leader. He was respected for being reasonable and fair but not for pulling his punch. Even those he criticized said as much. The public knew how strong the paper was, but few knew the private man.

After Gannett bought the Advertiser and a corporate replacement was brought in, Bill completed his workaday career on the editorial page staff. And another side of the man came before readers. His personal columns, so different from the political reporting and the persistent, if ineffectual, editorials, scolding Alabama politicians for their sin and follies, attracted a different set of readers, or perhaps readers weary of those sins and follies.

And along about here Yellow Cat entered my life. I followed that feline through all of his mishaps and was always happy when he again survived another scrape. Bill's essays without Yellow Cat were engaging, but that cat was always somewhere, out there in the bushes, watching and waiting, not one to miss a free meal but ever independent. He was a four-legged Huck Finn.

I am not reading too much into Yellow Cat in saying that he was the embodiment of Bill Brown's public. Yellow Cat was the student or young reporter who needs guidance but resists submission, the politician who wonders how he or she is coming across, the solitary reader who wants to know what the government is doing or not doing and hiding out to mull it over.

Now Yellow Cat, wherever he is, cannot tell us how much he appreciates Bill Brown's concern for his welfare. He is not the young reporter who bridled at Bill's direction and, much later in life, wrote to thank him for instruction she could not have known would shape her into a successful journalist. But what Yellow Cat cannot, probably would not, say, we who have read, and now, with pleasure, re-read, can. And so will those meeting Yellow Cat and his alter ego for the first time.

As a regular reader of Bill Brown's columns, I can say that they are worth binding in a volume, because they elevate our calling and our compassion. They are carefully crafted, full of insights and good humor, and, in the best sense, entertaining. They also reveal the mind and the heart of a journalist who can write about the roughest patches in life and, still, through some miraculous gift, lift our spirits.

Jerry Elijah Brown
Professor and Dean, Emeritus
The University of Montana

Introduction

The yellow cat—later known as Yellow Cat—is largely responsible for this book. Of all the persons, creatures and things I have written about, Yellow Cat had the largest and most vocal following. If I had not reported on Yellow Cat's doings for a while, people whom I did not know would come up to me in the grocery store and inquire about his well being. After Yellow Cat's death, other strangers would express regret.

When Yellow Cat came into my life—was coaxed into my life would be a more accurate description—I did not know that I would write about him at all, much less as often as I did. You might note from the cover photo that YC looks more orange than yellow, but in his days as a down-and-outer he was skinny and unkempt and he looked more yellow than he did after he became prosperous. So Yellow Cat stuck; it rolls off the tongue more easily than Orange Cat, anyway.

This volume also came about because I am a packrat. Not quite one of those hoarders you see on TV, I do tend to keep stuff as long as I can find a place to put it. That goes for anything from a handful of screws left over from a project to items torn from newspapers to letters.

Experience has taught me that if you pack something up and move it, you will keep it many more years. So, anticipating that sometime in the coming months we will move to smaller digs (downsize is the trendy description), I have been sorting out and cleaning out. I have given stacks of books to the Friends of the Dadeville Public Library for their book sales. I always have to handle a book three or four times before I can persuade myself that I can part with it. I've carted away clothing that I hadn't worn in years, and there's more that I should get rid of.

Most of the stuff is unremarkable, but a few file folders stuffed with letters brought the cleaning out to a temporary halt. Most were in response to something I had written. Some were on letterhead stationery and had been dictated; others were in ink on monogrammed note cards or scrawled in pencil or ballpoint pen on sheets torn from a pad of paper or a spiral notebook.

The letters reminded me of something I already knew. If I thundered about some current issue, (and I could thunder pretty good), I would hear from a handful of the politically active. If I wrote about the cat who became my ward, I got letters from as far away as Newfoundland. When I wrote about our region's colorful expressions, I heard from people in Alaska and Australia.

Many of the letters shared a memory or experience that something I'd written had stirred. Some said, "You wrote what I had been thinking but had not put into words."

A note that I particularly treasured said simply, "Mr. Brown, I just wanted you to know how much I enjoyed your stories. Instead of reading, I felt like you were telling me a story."

Stories—both hearing them and telling them—were always a part of my life. I remember making up stories to entertain my sister and our cousins as we lay on pallets in the living room of my grandparents old farm house.

Later, I used an aunt's portable typewriter to produce a neighborhood newspaper. I don't recall whether there was a second issue; it was pretty labor intensive.

When I rode my bicycle to town as a kid, I would go in the side door of our little local newspaper and stand watching the news from all over churn out of the lone wire service teletype machine. A retiree who had been a foreign correspondent wrote a column for the paper about his adventures. I eagerly devoured every word. The big cabinet radio in the hall at my grandparents' house was used only on Saturday nights to tune in the Louisiana Hayride and the Grand Old Opry. I discovered it had several short wave bands, and I would twirl around the dial, listening to news broadcasts from stations around the world. The static just added to the adventure.

In truth, there wasn't much I wasn't interested in. My cousin's grandfather dubbed me The Wizard because I was always experimenting with things. I figured out how to hot wire my grandfather's old Studebaker truck long before my cousins and I could legally drive. It was hardly necessary since the keys were always on the mantle, but it was still exotic. I learned how to connect a set of headphones to the telephone wires so we could listen in on people talking on our party line. We knocked off doing that before Ma Bell found us out.

I gave some fleeting thought to becoming an engineer, but high school algebra disabused me of that notion. My high school bookkeeping teacher urged me to consider becoming an accountant. A great aunt urged me to become a pharmacist.

None of that appealed, and looking back, I don't know how I could have done anything but journalism.

Writing, if you are serious about it, is hard work, and it is gratifying to succeed occasionally. Anyone who writes is exposing himself in one way or another, and it took some years to find that the things I enjoyed writing about most were those personal stories that drew a response from real human beings.

I subscribe to E.B. White's observation that the essayist is "sustained by the childish belief that everything he thinks about, everything that happens to him, is of general interest."

Later, when I was writing personal essays more often, I learned how to judge when a piece was likely to draw a greater than usual response. It was when my best editor, who happens to be my wife, would raise an eyebrow and wonder whether I was making too much of a small thing. Life, though, consists of small things punctuated occasionally by some monumental event. In the cosmic order, learning to live with a new wallet, trying to outwit a squirrel or experiencing the joy of lingering in the hammock are small potatoes. But they are potatoes we all have dined on.

Reading the letters in those file folders prompted me to reexamine several decades worth of writing.

Much that I had written was about transitory things, current topics written more with deadlines in mind than in permanence, now as brittle as the newsprint they were printed on.

But there remained pieces that time had been kinder to, ones that stirred a memory or an emotion.

I have resisted the temptation to tinker very much with them. They were written over a period of time, and each had been written to stand on its own (you learn in journalism never to assume that the reader is familiar with earlier coverage of the same subject). In those pieces with a recurring theme, I have tried to eliminate some of the repetition while leaving enough to make them coherent, even if you skip around, something I encourage you to do. I also made the gender of Yellow Cat (who crops up regularly in these pages) consistent. Before we came to trust each other, I thought that YC was a female and some of the earlier pieces reflected that. It was only after YC paid a visit to the vet that I learned that he was a male that probably had been neutered at an early age.

Some of these essays appeared originally when I was an editor at the Columbus, Ga., Ledger-Enquirer and at the Montgomery, Ala., Advertiser. I am grateful to the editors at those papers for permitting me to use them here. The pieces that appeared in those newspapers are so noted.

Bill Brown
at Lake Martin

Moral Lessons at the Movies

July 1998

WE DIDN'T KNOW we were being exposed to moral lessons. We thought we were just watching exciting movies. I'll bet the guys who were in those movies, Roy Rogers and Gene Autry, were more interested in entertaining us than in imparting lessons.

Gene Autry is still with us at 90. Roy Rogers died Monday at 86, still the King of the Cowboys.

Our arguments about them weren't about the nature of good and evil. They were about who was the best cowboy, the best good guy.

How those arguments raged.

"Roy Rogers is the best."

"You're crazy. Gene Autry is the best."

"Well, Roy Rogers is the King of the Cowboys."

"He wouldn't be if Gene Autry hadn't gone off to fight in the war. He let Roy Rogers be king while he was gone."

The disputes—the kind that are never settled—usually began on the way to the Saturday afternoon matinee. You could see a cowboy

9

movie, maybe a serial like Superman, and a cartoon, all for a dime.

They continued after the movie until the topic was temporarily worn out. The partisans would restate their cases next week; no one would be swayed.

There were other cowboy movies stars, of course: Lash LaRue, Bob Steele, Hopalong Cassidy.

But those guys were the Royal Crown Colas of the movie world. Roy Rogers and Gene Autry were the Cokes. Nobody had anyone but Rogers or Autry at the top of their favorites list.

Even when a diehard Autry fan—that would be me—revealed to his buddies that Roy Rogers' real name was Leonard Slye and that he was from Ohio, it didn't make a difference with any of the Rogers fans, who outnumbered the Autry adherents by a wide margin. There must have been thousands, maybe millions, like them, because from 1943 to 1954 Rogers was the No. 1 western star at the box office.

No one could argue that the plots of his movies were especially memorable. You could pretty much count on the bad guys seeming to get the upper hand, Roy to have his back to the wall but to persevere. He eventually won and rode away on his trusty horse, Trigger, with Dale Evans by his side. Somewhere along the way he got to sing.

The bad guys were really evil, but Rogers always fought fair. Instead of killing the bad guys, he shot the gun out of their hands.

Regardless of the sameness of the plots, they kept us glued to our seats, movie after movie. We knew Roy was going to win; we wanted to see how.

Actually, the plots of all of them could be summed up simply: An appealing character strives against great odds to achieve a worthwhile goal.

In some part of our minds we already knew that life wasn't

always fair and that the good guys didn't always win, at least not in the short run.

But we learned that life ought to be fair and that good people should try to make it that way.

The cynical will argue that those are simply myths, but myths are powerful things that not only help explain our behavior but also shape it. The ancient Greeks and Romans understood that well.

I'm not sure what kind of lessons today's entertainment is teaching kids, but I'm glad I learned some of mine from the man in the white hat. And it's a comfort to know that somewhere out there on some cable channel Roy Rogers is still bringing the bad guys to justice and kids are still watching.

Montgomery Advertiser

Stealing Freedom

THE GASOLINE NOZZLE at the service station didn't have one of those automatic shutoffs, so while I filled the gasoline tank I asked my wife to clean the windshield. The morning sun had highlighted how dirty it really was.

There were a couple of those black plastic containers attached to posts by the gas pumps, the kind that usually hold some sort of grungy windshield cleaner solution and have a worn squeegee stuck in them. She looked in one, then the other: No squeegee.

She stepped inside the station to ask.

"We don't have any," the woman behind the counter said. "People keep stealing them." She did lend my wife a spray bottle of Windex and a roll of paper towels, so the windshield did get cleaned.

When I went in to pay for the gasoline, I sympathized. "People keep stealing the squeegees, huh?"

"Yeah, but that's not half of it. I work in a doctor's office. We used to have six wheelchairs in the waiting room for people to use to bring patients in from their cars. Now we have two. People wheel someone out and then just stick the wheelchair in their car trunk."

Not half indeed. Not even a fraction.

Our neighborhood grocery store has one of the crummiest collections of shopping carts I've ever seen. If you find one on which all four wheels roll, you don't complain about it being dented or rusty.

Some of the people in the neighborhood were complaining to each other about the situation—not only shopping carts, but the general condition of the store and the lack of variety in the merchandise. The idea came up briefly of sending a delegation to talk with the store's management.

One of the people involved in the discussion called things to a halt, though, with a bit of her inside knowledge.

"That store has the highest theft rate of any of their stores," she said. "They're not going to pour a bunch of money into it." The implication was that we're fortunate to have the store at all.

This, despite the fact that an off-duty policeman works at the store most of the time.

We all worry about violent crime, the kind that grabs the major headlines. Really, though, most of us aren't going to fall victim to it, and despite the perception, statistics show it is dropping.

What has changed our lives in many ways is the annoying, almost petty crime that has almost become accepted as a norm. The thefts themselves may be small potatoes, but what they've robbed us of is a sense of security and freedom.

There always have been people who stole things, but many of us who grew up in small towns can remember riding our bicycles to the movies and leaving them unlocked out front while we caught the Saturday afternoon matinee. And our bicycles were there when we came out.

We recall grandparents who, when they were away from home, confidently left the front door locked to let everyone know they were gone and the back door unlocked in case anyone needed anything.

Now even country homes have burglar bars, and mercury vapor lights have become so ubiquitous that they blot out the stars miles out in the country. We who live in town have learned to lock the doors, even if we're only in the back garden, and we don't leave the granddaughter's tricycle sitting out in the front yard overnight.

Jimmy Buffet and his buddies weren't the only guys running through the minimart stuffing things in their jeans.

A young man I know worked nights—often alone—in a liquor store. The company that owned the store apparently just considered theft a cost of doing business and didn't invest in a second employee or even a security camera.

He tried to stay vigilant, but there were times he was certain people were stealing. When someone walks in wearing a jacket in the hot summer, you figure he's not having a chill or making a fashion statement.

The young man had been taught that stealing is wrong, and it pained him to watch someone walk out the door with a bottle of booze stuffed under his jacket. It also struck him as something less than brilliant to risk his life for a company that was unwilling to do more to stop it. He finally did the only thing he could; he quit.

They say that if you put a frog in a pot of boiling water, he'll hop right out, but if you start with cold water and heat it gradually, the frog will keep swimming around until you've boiled him.

It seems to me that the temperature has gradually been going up, and we're just swimming around.

Montgomery Advertiser

A Citizen of the World

January 2002

ON A COLD, raw day a couple of weeks ago, Hendry was waiting on the front porch when I stopped by home at lunchtime.

We had been expecting her.

Hendry, I should explain, is a cat. She belongs to our son's family, as much as a cat belongs to anyone. They got her when she was a tiny ball of fur. They thought the kitten was a male—it is hard to tell when they're small—and they named the kitten Henry. Only the granddaughter, Nora, couldn't say Henry, so it became Hendry. By the time they figured out Hendry was a girl, the name had stuck.

Hendry grew up next door to us in Montgomery's Capitol Heights. She was accustomed to coming and going as she pleased.

Then, last summer, Hendry's family bought a home in Dalraida, about 2 1/2 miles away from us. They did not consult Hendry about their decision.

They did all the things one does when moving pets. They kept her inside for days so she could get accustomed to her new home.

But Hendry is a cat that loves the outdoors, and eventually her demands for freedom were granted.

For a few days she seemed content to explore her new environs, but then she disappeared.

It took a week for her to get to Capitol Heights. Crossing Dalraida Road, Coliseum Boulevard and Federal Drive wasn't much of a challenge. By coincidence, our son was visiting with us when Hendry marched up to our front door, demanded admission and let it be known that she was hungry. She didn't really look any the worse for wear, although she'd been on the road, so to speak. Her trip home with our son took no more than 10 minutes.

It took longer for Hendry to win outdoor privileges this time. It didn't matter.

The second trip was quicker. Only a couple of days after she disappeared from her owners' home, she was back at ours.

Our daughter-in-law retrieved her, as she did the next time.

Back in Dalraida, Hendry was as confined as a prisoner doing hard time. But most prisoners, including Hendry, eventually breathe free air.

The fourth time Hendry came back, her family was at our house. We were sitting in the living room that very late autumn day. The front door was partially open to the screen porch, which has a pet door. As we talked, the heavy door opened wider and in came Hendry. She had time for only a quick inspection tour before she was loaded in the car and driven home.

Just as snow clouds were heading toward Alabama, Hendry was again heading toward Capitol Heights.

This trek took longer. We'd been alerted that she had disappeared, and we were keeping an eye out for her. We were beginning to worry that the 2.4 miles (that's got to be a lot of little cat steps) had been too hazardous this time. Perhaps the snow confused her navigation system; we hoped that she had just found some warm refuge to wait it out until the weather improved.

Nonetheless, before the last of the snow melted, she was there on the front porch as if the place were her home.

We hadn't rewarded her past treks by allowing her into the house; we thought we might preserve the idea that this wasn't her home.

Obviously it had not worked, and this time it was cold.

And I had actually bought a couple of cans of cat food anticipating that we hadn't seen the last of her.

So when I opened the door, she sauntered in.

She stayed at the dish of food until it was empty. Then she curled up next to one of the heat registers. Cats do love comfort.

We have invited Hendry to go back to her family. When we leave for the weekend, we put her outside with access to the porch where there is food, water and a box with an old blanket in it. Thus far, Hendry has been there when we return.

We don't fool ourselves that Hendry keeps coming back to Capitol Heights because she is fond of us. She comes because she thinks this is her house.

Cats were a part of our household for most of our married life, but when our last cat disappeared, we decided we did not want another one.

With cats, you're not always the one who decides.

No matter whether she hangs around, though, Hendry is not our cat.

As our 7-year-old granddaughter, Nora, says grandly, "Hendry's not our cat; Hendry is the world's cat."

Montgomery Advertiser

Cheers Without the Booze

October 2002

PICTURE CHEERS without the booze. Nearly every small town has a spot like that, a place where people really do know your name, or at least your face.

In Dadeville, it's Bob's Fine Food. Bob's—whose owner actually is Michael—seats about 30 people. It's the kind of place where one of the regulars refills everyone's coffee cups if Valarie, usually the only waitress at breakfast, has her hands full.

If there are no empty booths, strangers are invited to share a table where there's a vacant seat. They remain strangers only if they choose to.

Places like Bob's are among the things that make small towns special. There is a pace and familiarity to life that has a human dimension. You can forget about communicating with the person across the building by e-mail or trying to figure out which number to select when you're ensnared in a telephone tree. It's a lot less stressful to get caught up in the town's rush minute instead of a rush hour.

Even so, moving to a small town—and figuring out that's where we want to be—was something of a surprise. When I went away to college, I thought I was saying goodbye to small town life forever,

18

and I was glad of it. Living in medium-sized and larger cities came with the career I had chosen, and we found things to appreciate in every city.

In fact, we didn't set out to leave Montgomery. We were simply looking for a convenient place on the water where we could unwind and where the kids and grandkids could play.

But Dadeville came along with that package, and it simply grew on us.

It took a while. We were deeply involved in Montgomery, and the lake was only for weekends—at least for the near term. But our neighbors were all full-time residents, and since we were there most weekends, we found a church to join. Without really planning it, we found ourselves increasingly involved in the community.

So a few weeks ago we capitulated and moved the last of the furniture from town.

In doing so, we found that we had followed the path others had trod. They came because of the water but gradually realized that this was where they wanted to be. There's also a healthy sprinkling of people who grew up here and spent careers all over the country, never expecting to see Dadeville again. But here they are.

They're not just retirees. The circle includes people in mid career who are willing to trade the commute to Auburn, Montgomery or Birmingham for the amenities of a small town.

Lake Martin is a plus for Dadeville, but when you ask people why they've chosen to live here, the water isn't at the top of the list.

The attraction, they say, is that in a small town you feel like a real person. You don't just see people in one context. You see the bank president working alongside volunteer prisoners from the county jail building a playground for the community's kids. You see the grocery store owner dishing up food at a fund raiser for a local cause. That kind of familiarity encourages a certain amount of civility, too. It's more difficult to be rude to—or dishonest with—someone you're likely to see every time you turn around.

Even the most avid small town booster will admit that some are closed societies that shut out newcomers. But I think you pretty much find what you expect to find, and there are people just waiting for the chance to welcome you.

In celebrating life in a small town, I am not denigrating cities. In fact, living in a small town gives us a greater appreciation of the variety and stimulation a city has to offer. Better roads mean that most small towns aren't as isolated as they once were. It's no big deal to drive in to town to eat out, take in a movie or go shopping. But it is with pleasure that we top the hill and see glowing in the headlights the street sign that tells us we are home.

It has been said that familiarity breeds contempt.

It can also breed contentment.

Sense Ain't Common

June 2004

THERE ARE DAYS when I suspect that rules have triumphed over common sense.

Having rules is a price we pay for living in an organized society. But sometimes walking around sense seems to have sat down.

An accumulation of events brings on this notion. Election Day helped to reinforce it.

Ours is a small town. One of the poll workers was a person whom I see in church almost every Sunday. We have attended social events in each other's homes.

Still, I couldn't get my ballot until I produced a picture ID.

I didn't take it personally; she was just following the rules. She said she'd have to ask her own husband for identification.

There's a good reason for making certain that voters are who they say they are. But in this case the insistence that poll workers check a picture ID seemed to me to be another example of paying more attention to following the rules than to accomplishing what the rules were created for in the first place.

It has gotten to where I rarely carry a pocket knife anymore, even though I've always found one to be useful for such mundane tasks as opening an envelope, clipping an interesting item from the paper, or cutting a loose thread.

I can't remember exactly when I got my first pocket knife—some time during grade school. Putting my knife in my pocket was part of my morning routine from then until a few years ago.

Now the small knife I've had for more than 20 years remains on top of the chest of drawers, with extra change and spare pens, unless I'm certain that I'm not going anyplace where carrying it would be considered suspicious. Going to an airport or a federal courthouse? A school?

Better to be safe than sorry.

Better safe than sorry is, of course, the reason we have so many rules.

Want to avoid a lawsuit? Make a rule and enforce it across the board, even it if doesn't make sense. Ours is a litigious society that often rewards people for their own stupidity.

And if you have a rule, you don't have to accept responsibility for making a judgment. "Sorry, I'd like to help, but there are rules."

Take the case last week in West Jordan, Utah, where a 13-year-old student was suspended for 45 days for giving a cousin a cold pill —even though the medication had been prescribed for both of them.

In Jefferson County not long ago, a Clay-Chalkville High School student was suspended for a month and sent to an alternative school for taking a Motrin tablet for cramps. Still, she was luckier than a Bossier City, La., high school student who was expelled for a year for having Advil at school.

Sometimes zero tolerance makes zero sense.

(These absurdities are reminders of the warning labels plastered all over every imaginable product. No matter how absurd a warning label you can imagine, there probably is a real one that is even more absurd—such as the one on a fishing lure that says "harmful if swallowed." Gee, why didn't we all get electrocuted before they attached the label warning us not to use the electric hair dryer in the shower?)

It's easy to get indignant about mindless rules that foreclose the application of common sense. I wonder, though, how many of us who chafe at such rules have had a hand in creating the same kinds of situations. Many of us, for example, have insisted on tough-on-crime sentencing laws that give judges little or no flexibility in making the punishment fit the crime.

Will Rogers observed a long time ago that "Common sense ain't common."

Think how much more rare it has gotten since his day.

Evidence of Our Existence

March 2003

PHYSICAL LABOR has a way of freeing the mind to roam, even to ponder such questions as immortality. As I was doing chores the other day, my thoughts wandered to my grandparents, long dead but never very far away.

As is so often the case, spring burst upon us after a stretch of weather that was too wet and too cold for outdoor work. So I labored away trying to make up for lost time, washing and sealing the decks, cutting brush, digging out space for a planting bed.

As I swung a shovel full of dirt, I was transported to childhood and to my grandparents' farm. Even as boys we—my cousin, my brother and I—were recruited to help out. They started as simple jobs: gathering the eggs, filling the wood bin or using the hand pump at the well by the barn to fill the water trough.

As we got bigger, so did the jobs. If the work involved moving dirt or clearing brush, we attacked the project full speed. We were, I guess, hoping to get finished quickly so we could play.

My grandfather, who was less than 6 feet tall and who probably didn't weigh more than 160 pounds, was more deliberate. Where our shovels were full, his contained only half as much.

But our arms hung heavy long before the job was finished, while he worked steadily away.

He wasn't one to lecture, but we eventually learned by example to pace ourselves and to stick to the job until it was done.

The lesson is only one of many that were imparted, though there are times that I have to remind myself of things I thought I had learned.

My grandmother taught a different, gentle kind of patience. When we had done something to set my grandfather off—such as putting a floor in the cupola of the hay barn, which could easily have caused a fire—it was my grandmother who interceded.

"Now, Mack," she said. "They're just boys."

It was a reminder that she would deliver often. I think of those words now that I have grandchildren of my own.

I thought about my grandparents on Sunday, too, as we attended the funeral of the matriarch of a family in our community.

Representing two of the family's four generations, a son and a grandson shared warm memories of a woman who nurtured, educated, entertained and loved not only her own family, but a far wider circle.

What she and my grandparents and countless others taught by word and, more importantly, deed, radiates far beyond their immediate circle, even to generations yet to come.

Most of us long to leave some evidence of our existence. The pharaohs did it with their pyramids. Modern business tycoons strew the landscape with buildings bearing their names (some of them built, we learn, with money that wasn't necessarily the tycoons' to give).

There is another, more personal way of leaving evidence of our passage through this world.

It is called love.

Waiting for Yellow Cat

March 2003

EVERY EVENING, about dark, Hendry bounds out of the door and sits on the step, looking expectantly toward the driveway.

She is waiting for the yellow cat.

Hendry is the cat that lives with us, although technically she belongs to our son and his family. She did not approve when her family moved from next door to us in Montgomery to a new home several miles away, so she kept returning to her old neighborhood. We moved Hendry to the lake when we took up full-time residence here last August and kept her inside for months to discourage her from trying to go back to Montgomery.

Heartworm is a threat to cats, so I went to a local veterinarian's office in late fall to get a fresh supply of heartworm pills. I told him about Hendry's adventures and that we were beginning to allow her to go outside.

He sounded a cautionary note. Possums and feral cats stake out territories, he said, and they could attack a newcomer. He suggested that we borrow a Havahart trap from the Humane Society and set it out during a time when Hendry was indoors.

26

If we caught a possum, we could release it out in the country, he said; a feral cat could be put down humanely.

I knew the vet was right, but I didn't tell him about the yellow cat. I admired his grit too much to be the one to sign his death warrant. (I never actually got close enough to determine the cat's sex, it seemed to be the size of a female. I was to learn later that yellow cat was a neutered male.)

I had been seeing the yellow cat off and on for more than a year. I would see him curled up in the sun at the end of our retaining wall or sitting under a bush down the hill from the house. He apparently covered a wide range. I had seen him in the woods by the boat ramp more than a mile from the house. Neighbors also reported seeing him.

He was skinny, and his fur was matted; he had luminous eyes. If anyone tried to come near, he disappeared into the bushes. Occasionally I had put out food, well away from the house. It disappeared, but I never knew whether it went into his stomach.

After Hendry came to the lake, sightings of the yellow cat increased even though Hendry remained indoors. It was as if the yellow cat sensed that ours might be a friendly place.

I put a food dish at the edge of our parking area, and he ate from it regularly. Eventually I moved it to the side deck, and he began appearing every evening, just about dark. I could watch him from the kitchen window or through the glass paneled door. He would wolf down a few bites, raise his head to look around for danger, and return to his meal. He nearly always emptied the dish.

Over the weeks he began to fill out. He still retreated if I stepped outside, but not so far anymore.

Hendry was outside one evening as darkness fell. Through the glass I saw her sitting on the railing of the side deck, feet tucked under her. I opened the door to see if she wanted to come in, but she just sat. I stepped out and looked around the corner. On the deck sat the yellow cat, his pose similar to Hendry's. They were simply gazing at each other. I stepped back inside.

A few evenings later I looked out. The yellow cat was eating ravenously; Hendry was nestled a few feet away, watching.

No matter where she was in the house, Hendry could hear me open the side door to put out the yellow cat's dish. She would rush out, sniff around the dish—though she never ate from it—and then curl up to wait. I never heard the two cats exchange sounds, but they seemed to share a companionable silence. After the yellow cat dined and departed, Hendry was ready to come inside.

A few weeks ago, the yellow cat stopped appearing, and I fear that something bad has happened.

But every evening Hendry asks to go out and waits on the step, looking expectantly toward the driveway.

What the Good Teachers Had

May 2003

PERHAPS IT'S BECAUSE the students in the course I taught at Auburn University in Montgomery this spring were education majors that I spent some time thinking about the impact that teachers had on my life.

The students in my class are preparing to be high school English teachers. They were taking the journalism class because it's usually an English teacher who is tapped to be adviser to the school newspaper.

During our first class meeting, I told the students I was pleased to try to help them prepare for their calling because it was a way of repaying some of the teachers who did so much for me.

I had not just one or two outstanding teachers, I told the class, but a whole list of them, from elementary school on. The list would include all four of my high school English teachers, an unusually lucky thing for someone who would go on to spend a career working with words.

One of the students had a question: What did those good teachers have in common?

I had to stop and think. They were so different in appearance, personality and style. Of the high school English teachers, there was only one that I was truly fond of. It was only after I went off to college that I realized how well they all had prepared me for the next step. Of course, I had taken advantage of what they had to offer, but they had something to do with that, too.

What those teachers had in common, I think, was that they treated their students as if they were important. They also treated their students as if they had walking around sense.

That doesn't mean that those teachers spent a lot of time with warm fuzzy praise trying to make us feel good about ourselves. They spent a lot of time pushing us to learn and treating us as if we were capable of learning. If we succeeded at that, self-esteem came as a result.

For many kids, that positive expectation was enough to spur them to greater effort so that they wouldn't disappoint the person who believed in them.

Interesting, isn't it, how often we perform to the level that is expected of us, not only in school, but in life. Interesting, too, how often the people in charge of things, including schools, seem to forget that.

All was not rosy in those classrooms, despite our predilection for viewing the past through a soft focus lens that hides its imperfections.

Social promotion was a fact of life; kids who weren't "normal" but who weren't behavioral problems just occupied space in the same classrooms as their age group. Kids who wouldn't or couldn't conform were hounded out of school as soon as they were old enough to quit. Other kids quit trying long before they could leave. I'm sure that even the teachers who were so good for many of us wrote most of those kids off.

If things weren't perfect, they weren't terribly bad. Drugs weren't even on our radar screen; even the experimenting with alcohol was limited. The closest thing we saw to violence was a couple of gland-ridden teens going at each other with their fists. And in any disagreement between teachers and students, parents were more likely to side with the teachers than sue them.

Our society has changed in so many ways that the challenges are more difficult now, I think, for teachers and for students.

I don't know how many of the students who were in my class this spring will go on to be teachers, but it is a comfort to know that there still are people who want to be teachers.

The best of them—the ones who treat students as if they are important and who instill a desire in their students to live up to expectations—will have a far greater impact than they could ever imagine.

But I Liked the Old One

January 2001

THE NEW WALLET sat on the chest of drawers for a week before I decided that the time had finally come.

I had known even before I unwrapped the Christmas gift what it was. The size and shape of the box practically cried wallet.

And it was. Rich brown leather. Name brand. Well made.

It was just what I needed. The only thing wrong with it was that it was new.

I had written last April that I was going to have to face up to the fact that my old wallet—I can't recall how long I'd had it—was falling apart and I needed a new one.

Of course I didn't face up to the fact at all. I simply got rid of some of the excess baggage the wallet held and kept on carrying it. I never seemed to have time to go shopping for a new one.

Christmas removed that excuse.

When I laid my wallet down next to the new one every evening, the old looked like the country cousin come to town.

New Year's Day seemed like a good time to deal with the inevitable, so I emptied my old wallet, spreading its contents across the bedspread. It was like emptying a clown car.

It seemed as if it had been only a few weeks since I had cleaned it out. When I spread it out, though, there was a lot of stuff in the crumbling package of leather.

A discount store card.

Four credit cards, including one from a department store where I rarely shop and which accepts general purpose credit cards anyway.

Driver's license.

Auto insurance card.

Health insurance card.

Dental insurance card.

A foldover card with a summary of company benefits.

Bank account card.

Piece of paper with my wife's clothing sizes (a holdover from Christmas shopping).

A scrap of paper with several telephone numbers.

Four old credit card receipts.

Five bills—all small.

The pile was only marginally smaller than the one I'd made when I thinned out its contents back in April. At least there weren't any pieces of paper with scribbled notes I couldn't read or telephone numbers that I had no recollection of.

All the stuff wouldn't fit into the new wallet.

Not even after I threw away the credit card receipts and entered the list of sizes, telephone numbers and e-mail addresses into my electronic organizer.

So I stuck some of the other things in a drawer.

At last I got everything into the new wallet.

The credit cards felt strange sliding into the pockets, almost as if the pockets were too small. I'm sure that I'll need something that I threw away; I'll probably forget where I put the other things.

But I'll get by.

Eventually, I will throw the old wallet away, but for the moment it sits in a drawer. You don't rush into discarding things that have served you well.

The old wallet had taken on the shape of the part of my body it rested on, so that I didn't even have to look at it to know which direction to fit it into my pocket.

The new wallet has not adapted to me—nor I to it—so that I have to look to put it in my pocket the same way every time.

Eventually it will conform.

And at some point—who can see that many years into the future?—I will have a difficult time deciding that its time is up.

Montgomery Advertiser

A Lifetime in 15 Minutes

December 1980

THE LITTLE KID was scared. He sat there in the middle of the family room floor, clutching his brother's hunting knife and straining to hear some sign that the intruder who surely was lurking in one of the darkened bedrooms was coming for him.

There was a telephone in the well lighted kitchen just a few steps away, but the intruder might hear his whispered call. Better just to sit very still. Lucky he had carried his brother's knife to the Cub Scout meeting to learn safety with knives.

It had started with one of those complications so typical of modern life.

Dad had to rush home from work, grab a quick bite and go to a meeting.

The 12-year-old's YMCA basketball team was practicing that night. The 9-year-old had a scout meeting that wouldn't be over until after 7.

Mom realized in mid-afternoon that her evening class would run late and the house might be empty when the 9-year-old got home from scouts. She called to suggest that he stay at his scout friend's house until she got home.

35

But it was a sunny day, and there were no shadows to hide unknown terrors. The only sounds were birds and children and the everyday creaks and groans that a house makes.

No, Mom, he didn't need to stay with anyone. He'd take his brother's house key with him and he'd be just fine until she got home.

By the time scouts was over, it was dark. The kids in the car knew he was going home to an empty house, and it was an invitation.

"What if the phone rings and someone says, 'I know you're there alone'?"

"What if someone's hiding in the bedroom?"

It doesn't take much to set the imagination of a 9-year-old racing. His heart was already pounding as the car turned up the steep driveway. Wait, there's Dad's car. Fear dropped away like dead leaves.

He waved goodbye to his friends.

Then he saw the note taped to the front door. He read it slowly in the glow of the front porch light.

"I walked to church. Call me at this number if you need me before Mom gets home. Dad." A telephone number was written below.

At least someone had left the lights on.

Fear was waiting in the corner to seize him.

He was trapped. The warm friendly house had turned sinister. There were rappings and tappings and groans he'd never heard before.

Every sound was a threat, every minute an eternity. He'd like to close his eyes to shut out the terror, but he couldn't make himself do that. He had to look after the house.

The headlights from an automobile swept up the drive, pushing fear back into its corner. The sounds became comforting ones, the thump of a car door closing, the clicking of a key into a lock.

Mom recognized the look, and it brought a flood of memories. She remembered the seeming hours of lying with covers pulled over her head, not daring to breathe because her sister had convinced her that fierce Indians standing in the corner of the room couldn't find her if she didn't breathe. Dad shivered a little as he recalled the hours he had cowered in a bathtub when he'd come home to an empty flat after a scary movie.

The 9-year-old, secure now in adult company, checked out each room of the house. Nothing there. And those sounds were just normal household sounds.

Still, he didn't want to spend 15 minutes like that again. Not anytime soon.

Columbus Ledger–Enquirer

You're Not My Pal

February 2002

WHEN WAS THE last time you and your spouse, or you and a party of friends, were addressed by the new collective, "you guys"?

I'd guess that it was the last time you ate at what is now called a casual dining establishment. If you're, say, 50 or older, you may have felt a tinge of resentment at being addressed with that kind of false familiarity by someone young enough to be your child or grandchild. If you did, you weren't alone.

I really hadn't thought about it much until a friend, who may be more of a curmudgeon than I, wrote about it in his magazine. He doesn't like it, and he particularly doesn't like it when a server (we dare not call them waiters or waitresses anymore) calls him by his first name when he pays by credit card.

The responses he got—and the ones I got in my casual inquiries —indicated that the false familiarity of "you guys" has irritated a nerve if not rubbed it raw.

I guess I had just put it down as one of those changes that society has made without consulting me. A lot of other people feel that they weren't consulted either.

Those of us who are, shall we say, more mature, may have encouraged all this. We don't dress the way our parents did when they were our age, and we don't act the way our parents did at our age. I can't imagine my father or grandfather wearing a pair of cutoffs, a tee shirt and a pair of boat shoes with no socks, but I see people my age dressed in much the same wardrobe as those a generation or two younger.

I've learned to live with "you guys," although I confess that "you all" or even "y'all" falls softer upon the ears. I do, however, wish that restaurants would knock off having their servers introduce themselves by name, as if we're going to be buddies. If the server insists on doing so, I listen, if only so I can call the person by name as he or she passes by, studiously avoiding looking in my direction, while my tea glass stands empty. I'd much rather get my needs met without having to call out at all. At one time that's what waiters and waitresses were there for.

Among those I've questioned, the spread of "you guys" is seen as only one indicator of the demise of manners. They see it reflected in everything from the failure of sales clerks to say "thank you" or "you're welcome" after a transaction to people talking on their cell phones in the movie theater.

A lack of courtesy is also reflected in the calls from telemarketers who insist on using what they think is your first name as if you were old friends.

When someone I don't know addresses me as William over the telephone, I hang up. I've never been called William by anyone except my mother, and when she called me that she usually had her hands on her hips and steel in her voice.

We curmudgeons regard false heartiness as condescending. We don't want to be treated as if we're doddering old fools who have to be addressed loudly and in single syllable words. But we don't want to be treated like everyone's buddy, either.

Good manners, it seems to me, are a lubricant that eases the every day interaction between people.

It seems, too, that familiarity in a relationship is something that takes time to develop.

It's a lot more pleasant for someone to address you as Mr. Smith or Mrs. Jones and have you ask them to call you by your first name than for them to call you Jack or Linda and have you say, "Mr. Smith to you."

An unsettling question lingers, though. If our generation doesn't dress like our parents did and doesn't act like our parents did, is it possible that we didn't raise our children with the same ideas about manners as our parents did?

Words That Made You See

October 2002

THERE WEREN'T MANY photographs around my grandparents' house; the only one I recall clearly hung over the mantle in the front bedroom. It was a tinted photograph of my great-grandfather in his cavalry uniform. As far as I know, my grandparents never owned a camera.

Yet I grew up with mental pictures of many of my ancestors that were sharper than any photograph could have been. In my mind, I knew not just their faces but what kind of people they were.

I knew because I had heard about them, not just once but countless times over the years when family and kin sat around telling stories.

Those of us who were the youngest generation absorbed much about who we were and where we came from by listening to our elders. They weren't talking to educate us; they were entertaining each other. But the effect was the same. No doubt many of the stories were embellished, just as a caricature exaggerates even as it depicts a truth.

All of that came to mind on a recent Saturday evening in Selma as I sat listening to storytellers at the 24th annual Tale Tellin' Festival. If I hadn't been in an auditorium, I could just as easily have been sitting around the fireplace in the hall at my grandparents' old farmhouse.

Barbara McBride-Smith may have grown up in Waco, Texas, but her story about her mother's button box and the events that each button represented was universal. When Jim May of Woodstock, Ill., recalled with love and humor his mother's move to a nursing home, many of us felt a stab of recognition. Alabama's premier storyteller, Kathryn Tucker Windham's account of a special day shared with her father sent many to bright pages in their own memory books.

Most of Saturday's audience was older—people who grew up when telling stories was a part of almost any gathering—but the audience included younger people and even kids. All seemed to find something in the stories to stir memories or laughter.

There is an intimacy about the spoken story that reaches us in places that a book or a film doesn't. There is some chemistry between the audience and the teller—or tellers—that binds us together.

Perhaps that's why the art of storytelling has survived technology and is growing.

Garrison Keillor's folksy recitation of the week's events in Lake Woebegon on public radio's Prairie Home Companion gave listeners across America a new appreciation for a well told tale. All of us knew people just like the characters of his mythical Minnesota town.

When the first National Storytelling Festival was held in Jonesborough, Tenn., in 1973, only about 60 people were there, counting the storytellers. But the seed that was planted there fell on fertile ground, and storytelling festivals, organizations and workshops have sprung up around the country.

Windham, a driving force behind the Selma festival and a true Alabama treasure, closed the Saturday performance with a plea for people to turn off the television, put down the video games and tell some stories.

I wonder whether we gave enough stories to our own children. Although our family ate supper together nearly every night without letting television intrude, the children didn't get to spend nearly enough time hearing stories from the older generation.

Time, distance, and even health were barriers, and our kids missed hearing their grandfather talk about growing up in rural North Louisiana when automobiles were an uncommon sight.

We tried to compensate for that by giving my late father-in-law a tape recorder and urging him to tell some of his stories to the microphone.

Unfortunately, he was one of those people who could barely change a light bulb, much less operate a tape recorder. After he died, my wife and her sister were going through his belongings. My wife found a cassette tape and popped it into a tape player. All that was on it was the exasperated voice of her father saying, "This blankety-blank thing doesn't work."

But we've had family adventures of our own.

Our children and grandchildren will have tons of pictures to chronicle their history, some printed on paper, some stored on a computer drive or whatever the technology devises.

I hope they will have some stories, too.

Invisible as Well as Silent

November 2002

I BELONG TO a generation that you rarely hear about.

Sandwiched between the GI generation—the one Tom Brokaw labeled the Greatest Generation—and the large, and often self-absorbed Baby Boom generation, we are the so-called "Silent Generation." Like the middle child in a family, we are ignored while the older and younger kids get all the oohs and aahs. The 2000 census counted 616,279 of us in Alabama.

We don't disagree with the accolades showered on the GI Generation, and we have to recognize the economic and cultural clout that size gives to the Boomers. But we don't like being invisible.

Born between 1925 and 1942, the older of us were children during the Great Depression, and the younger of us formed our first memories during World War II. If either of those major events made an impression upon us, it was mainly because of their effect on our parents.

We were solid—some would say stolid—citizens who could only look on with a combination of dismay and envy when the Boomers began rewriting the rules that we had grown up with.

Perhaps we've been overshadowed because there were only 49 million of us, the second smallest generation of the 20th century.

In contrast, the GI Generation, claimed 63 million. The Baby Boomers justified their label with a staggering 79 million.

Perhaps we've been ignored because we didn't make waves. Whoever labeled us the "Silent Generation"—several are given credit—hit the mark. We tended to be cautious. Some of that may have been a legacy from our parents, but the tenor of the times didn't encourage sticking your neck out.

While many of us were in grade school, nuclear war seemed to be a real possibility. We were the kids who were taught to duck under our desks and cover our heads in the event of an attack. That made an impression. Our generation saw that a career could be ruined if there was even a hint that a person wasn't a 100 percent reliable, true blue American. And a handful of powerful people decided what a true American was.

If silence was not golden, it was at least safe.

Even as adolescents, we were the mildest of rebels. We drank and drove fast but in retrospect, most of us were pretty tame.

Our generation went to school, got married, had families and took jobs that we expected to keep for life. Going home to live with the folks after college or turning down a job just because it wasn't perfect didn't cross our minds. We didn't spend more than we made, and we believed that hard work and loyalty counted for something.

We were taught that life had rules, and we believed it. Perhaps that's why members of the Silent Generation were the real heart of the Civil Rights Movement. The rules we were taught reflected the American ideal of liberty and justice for all. When it was apparent that the rules we'd been taught were being violated, the Silent Generation set out to put it right. In that regard, the movement wasn't so much a revolution as an attempt to enforce the rules.

In many ways, our small generation was a bridge. We missed out on the heroics of the GI generation, and on the social revolution wrought by the generation that followed.

But we built the economy that gave security to both the older generation and the younger one.

And, somewhere along the way, we wondered whether we'd missed something. Like the Pirate in the Jimmy Buffet song, many of us concluded that we were over 40 victims of fate.

But we are still here, still kicking.

Sixty percent or so of us have reached retirement age, and many of the rest of us are taking the opportunity to retire early. We are not content simply to sit on the porch but are striking out in new directions, traveling down some of the paths we didn't take earlier.

Perhaps we're revisiting the adolescence that we hurried through the first time around.

Life spans are increasing, and you may hear from us yet.

Bankrupt? Says Who?

December 2002

TUESDAY'S MAIL WAS the usual assortment of advertising circulars, catalogs, magazines and bills. There was also a letter from a national department store chain.

It didn't look like a bill, so I opened it as I stood there at the mailbox.

It was a perfunctory, computer-generated letter informing me that "Based on a review of your account, we are closing your account for the following reason: BANKRUPTCY FILING."

There was no signature. Under "sincerely" were the words "Credit Services" and a toll-free number.

By the time I got back to the house I was so mad I could spit, as my grandmother would say. I was glad I had taken my insurance physical that morning. I'm pretty sure my blood pressure reading at the moment would mean instant disqualification.

Certainly it was a mistake, meant for some other William Brown. But that was my address and account number on the flimsy paper.

I wanted answers. It would have been too much to expect a living person to answer the toll-free number, but it did seem reasonable to expect that the telephone tree would include an

47

option for dealing with the topic of the letter.

None of the three options did, so I picked one that seemed close, figuring that I would reach someone who could connect me to the right person. Instead, I got a recorded voice asking me to enter my Social Security number.

"Please wait while we access your account information," the voice said. It was followed by music, more "please wait" messages and more music.

At last a voice, still recorded, came on. "We are unable to locate your records," it said. It directed me to direct inquiries to a post office box in Arizona.

I couldn't wait that long. What would the next day's mail bring?

I called the company's Montgomery store. Another telephone tree—forest is more accurate. It listed 12 options before it came to "Credit Central."

A recorded female voice came on: "Please hold while I connect your call to an operator."

Of course, there was music. They always have music.

All the person in Montgomery could do—or seemed interested in doing—was give me a toll-free number for National Customer Relations.

Another telephone tree, another set of options. "Credit issues" seemed to describe the situation.

Another recorded voice told me that all representatives were "currently assisting other customers."

That message was followed by a string of commercials urging me to go out and use the credit card that the letter told me had been canceled.

At last a man who said his name was Tom came on. He couldn't explain why I had gotten the letter. "I do show a note that our bankruptcy department sent a letter, but I'm not showing where they closed the account."

He put me on hold while he contacted the bankruptcy department, and I was subjected to maddeningly peppy music as I waited.

Eventually a woman named Shannon, who used the word "actually" a lot (as in we actually don't give out our last name), was mystified, too. She had checked with the bankruptcy court in Alabama—presumably while I was listening to music—and nothing with my name on it showed up. Hold on, she said, and she would get an answer to why I had gotten the letter.

I was subjected to more music. When she came back on, she said, "Actually, we are going to be needing to do a little more research on this."

She called back. "Basically, what happened was, this was an error on our part and actually your account wasn't impacted with bankruptcy codes or credit bureaus ... it was just the letter went out in error.

"That would be an awful thing to get in the mail," she acknowledged, "and I would be shocked, too. ... I probably would have actually passed out." She assured me that the company had not sent out any derogatory information about my credit standing.

Maybe. But if they made the first mistake, couldn't they have made another? Personal finance experts tell us we ought to check our credit reports regularly. I've never bothered, but I certainly will now. Once information—even false information—gets into a database, it's hard to stamp it out, even more reason to worry about Adm. Poindexter's ambitious plan to develop dossiers on every American.

Meanwhile, Christmas shopping season is here. Like most Americans, we'll use plastic—except the national department store credit card we've had since before our children were born.

Round Goes to the Squirrel

December 2002

MAYBE IT'S TIME to yield the battlefield to the squirrel.

I've been on the verge of concession before, but this time I think I mean it. Not only has the squirrel taken the bird food, he's also taken the bird feeder.

The battle has been going on for a couple of years now.

I put up a bird feeder, placing it in a way that I thought would foil the squirrel. The squirrel—we have named him Jeff because his death defying aerial acrobatics are reminiscent of some of our older son's youthful exploits—was stymied for a while. He was persistent, though, and eventually he found a way to get at the treasure that I had dangled out of his reach.

After the last of several defeats nearly a year ago, I said I was giving up and put the feeder away.

In the past week or so, though, little birds have been flitting around our trees, and it seemed inhospitable not to offer them a welcome.

So I searched the utility room and found the feeder. It is made of vinyl-covered wire and is a little larger than a slice of bread. One side swings open so that a cake of suet can be inserted; the mechanism for keeping it closed seemed strong enough.

The sturdy handle, shaped like the handle on a syrup bucket, was missing. After Jeff's last success in freeing the feeder from its tether, I had found the feeder well away from the scene of the crime. The suet was missing, and so was the handle.

I fashioned a new handle from some heavy copper wire.

In the past, I suspended the feeder by a thin piece of cord from the slender limb of a tree by the front deck. We sat at the dining table watching Jeff try to get at the feast. He couldn't reach the feeder from the tree trunk, so he would venture onto the limb. He couldn't reach the feeder from there, either, not even hanging by his back legs. He would return to the tree trunk, think for a while, and then venture back onto the limb.

Then he disappeared. He had given up, I thought. I enjoyed the victory, and the birds enjoyed the suet.

We celebrated too soon.

Within a couple of days, the feeder disappeared. When I found it, I thought about tossing it—I didn't plan to hang it again—but it's not my nature to throw things away, and I put it on the shelf.

It took a while to find it when I decided to try again. This time I hung the feeder with even thinner cord from a tree in view of the kitchen window.

The squirrel never made an appearance while I was watching, but after a couple of days I looked out of the window and saw only a dangling white cord. The end of the cord was frayed, too frayed to have simply broken.   I'm guessing that it was chewed. What I would like to know is whether Jeff hoisted the feeder up to the tree limb to sever the cord at the handle or whether he took a leap and hung on while he chewed the cord. If so, what happened when the feeder came down, suet, squirrel and all?

I also wondered where he put the feeder. I walked a wide radius around the tree and didn't find it. High in a nearby tree there's a large nest. Did he cart it up there? It really doesn't matter, I guess.

A friend bought what is billed as a squirrel-proof feeder. Its platform is a wheel that begins spinning when something as heavy as a squirrel lands on it, launching the trespasser into space. My friend says he's seen it work.

He hasn't seen Jeff in action, though. In the battle of man versus squirrel, I'm ready to put my money on the squirrel.

What the Neighbors Think

April 2003

SPRING IS WELL upon us.

The pine pollen that gave everything a golden patina marked the beginning. The inner parts of my car—such as the insides of the door—still bear the evidence. Nothing short of a bucket of water and a rag will excise it.

Then came the catkins, raining down on driveways and decks and windshields. They cling tenaciously, and as soon as you finishing blowing them away, the breeze releases a fresh cascade.

Now the final confirmation that the season has arrived: The personal watercraft have returned to the lake—big time.

There is something Orwellian in the term personal watercraft. It calls up an image of an individual gliding serenely along, enjoying the peace of the outdoors. Nothing could be at more odds with what personal watercraft really are.

There is very little personal about them. They are shared by everyone within hearing distance regardless of whether they wish to be part of the experience.

It is only fair to acknowledge that noise is a part of being around the water. Pontoon boats ferry sightseers. Runabouts pull people on skis and tubes and kneeboards. Hyperactive fishermen roar past, fish for a few minutes, and then roar off again in search of a more productive spot.

The noise they make, though, pales in comparison to personal watercraft, particularly when there is a swarm of them. And only the personal watercraft seem to go in endless circles in a small geographic area.

I talked to a waterfront resident who likes to enjoy his paper and coffee in his gazebo on Sunday mornings. Unfortunately, at the time of year that's most pleasant for doing that, he has been driven indoors by the noise. Another waterfront couple I know takes a lot of weekend trips during the summer. They figure they can enjoy the water during the week, when it's often as quiet as a millpond. The husband enjoys fishing during the week, but he wouldn't dream of going out on the weekend.

We are among the lucky ones. On a recent Tuesday evening we motored out to the main river channel, cut the engine, and watched the sun set. There was only one other boat in sight.

For many people, though, the weekend is the only time they can seek the rejuvenation that being near the water brings. And they are having difficulty finding their moment of quiet.

The fact is, personal watercraft are fun, just as riding in a fast sports car or on a motorcycle is fun. As my son said once after borrowing my sports car, 'You know, it's real easy to be a jerk in that car."

I don't think that people out riding personal water craft—at least most of them—are deliberately trying to be jerks.

I think they get so absorbed in doing their own thing that they don't pay attention to the effect that they're having on others.

We are, after all, a pretty self-absorbed culture.

There are countless examples of our infatuation with our own pleasure and convenience to the exclusion of all else.

Some of us came out of a restaurant not long ago just behind a group of motor cyclists; I would hardly call them a gang. They started their engines, but they didn't leave right away, nor did they just let their engines idle. They wound them up until they shrieked (if they had mufflers, it was not evident), pleasing themselves and impressing each other, oblivious or indifferent to the fact that they were annoying the heck out of everyone else around.

They did that for what seemed an interminable time, and we gave up efforts to converse until they roared away one by one.

We are told of people who insist on talking on their cell phones in movie theaters, we see able people park in spaces reserved for the handicapped; we hear people conversing in gutter language in a grocery store checkout line.

We used to hear the question, "What will the neighbors think?" We often heard it from our parents when we were doing something they thought was outrageous.

Often the question was a bludgeon for enforcing conformity.

Now perhaps we don't hear it enough. Life might function a little more smoothly if all of us, at least occasionally, considered what the neighbors might think.

Waiting for the Call

April 2003

ON THE FRIDAY before Easter two years ago, I spent the day waiting for a telephone call that did not come. Deep inside, I knew what the caller would say. I just didn't know how I would handle it.

The clock passed 5, then 5:30. No call. I left the office knowing that it would surely come on Monday.

It all started five or six weeks earlier.

I didn't write down on the calendar the date that I caught a glimpse of a mole on my shoulder as I was toweling off. It had the angry look of one of those cancerous moles you see on a poster in the doctor's office. How long had it been there?

Fear clutched at my stomach.

My annual physical was due in a few weeks. I would show it to the doctor then and ask him what he thought. My wife the psychologist would call that denial, but I didn't want to tell her and have her get alarmed about something that might be nothing. She would call that self-delusion.

I didn't have to show the mole to the doctor. He spotted it right off. "We need to get a biopsy on this," he said. I guess he heard the alarm in his own voice, because he tried to soften it. "It's probably nothing," he said.

We both knew he was lying.

The biopsy was scheduled for a week later, a week of trying not to stare at my shoulder in the mirror, of trying not to think about what that dark dot could do to my life.

The doctor took the plug from my skin and said the pathology report might be back by Friday. He would call.

On the surface, it appeared to be an ordinary week with a full schedule of work and civic obligations. Inside, though, it wasn't an ordinary week at all. It was if I were standing outside myself watching somebody else go through life's daily rituals.

We had house guests for the Easter weekend, and I tried to be a good host. There was no need to put a damper on their weekend with my own fears.

I just wanted to get it over with—whatever it was.

The call came on Monday morning. My physician has always treated me as if I were a grownup, and he came right to the point. "It's a malignant melanoma." That's the deadliest of skin cancers.

I was sitting at my desk in an office I shared with two other people. I felt very much alone, and it was the one time I wished I'd been treated like a scared child. I needed someone's hand to hold.

"What do we do now?" I asked.

One of the top melanoma experts in the country was at the University of Alabama at Birmingham, he said. We could see about getting in there.

What about locally, I asked. Was there someone he would go to if he were in the same situation?

There was.

Make an appointment for as soon as they can see me, I asked.

Two days later, I excused myself from a civic board meeting that had dragged on past one o'clock and met my wife at the surgeon's office.

I had expected that we would talk about options, but within a few minutes I was face down on a table waiting for a local anesthetic to work. Minutes later the surgeon was cutting away what felt like a substantial part of my shoulder.

He sent the tissue he had removed to UAB.

The report was good, but the consultant recommended removing an extra margin to be on the safe side.

Take as much as you want, I said.

The second report came back even more promising. There were no residual cancer cells in the tissue.

The follow-up visits have been good, and the surgeon has stretched out the time between appointments.

I try to remember to wear a cap and sunscreen when I am outdoors, though that may be a case of locking the barn door after a good many of the horses have been stolen.

I try to recall the things that I thought about when I didn't know how the story might turn out. It wasn't the idea of missing possessions that wrapped me in sadness. The important things were experiences: the touch of someone you love, watching a grandchild grow up, watching the sun set and the moon rise, watching leaves tremble in a fresh breeze.

And I try to realize that every day is a gift to do with what we will.

Absent Without Explanation

May 2003

SINCE THE YELLOW CAT returned from his unexplained absence, Hendry doesn't find him to be nearly so charming. In fact, she regards the yellow cat with undisguised hostility.

Hendry is the cat that insisted on living with us when her real owners—our son and his family—moved from next door in Montgomery to a new home several miles away. When we moved last August from Montgomery to what had been our weekend home on Lake Martin near Dadeville, Hendry came along.

She has been content to be here.

The yellow cat was around the neighborhood long before Hendry's arrival, but after Hendry came into the picture, the yellow cat appeared near our house more often. After a while, the yellow cat began showing up every evening to scarf down a dish of food. Hendry often curled up only a couple of feet away and watched him eat. Occasionally the yellow cat curled up for a while before vanishing into the evening. Hendry seemed to regard him as one would a traveler from an exotic land.

Then one night the yellow cat failed to appear.

Days passed, then weeks, and I feared the yellow cat's luck had run out.

Hendry was not as pessimistic. She sat on the stoop every evening, looking expectantly toward the driveway.

Finally, one evening I saw Hendry sitting absolutely still on the stoop, staring toward the driveway.

Sometimes cats just stare into space, but I looked around the corner. The yellow cat sat in his usual spot, looking none the worse for wear and offering no explanation for his absence.

When he saw me, instead of retreating the yellow cat strode right up, rubbed against my leg and asked when dinner would be served.

I thought Hendry would be pleased to see him.

I was wrong. Hendry hissed and stalked inside.

Now the yellow cat shows up morning and evening. He sits staring through the glass door, and when I open it to put his dish out, he lets me know that he would be perfectly willing to come inside to eat.

The exotic traveler has now become the interloper, the potential rival. When Hendry sees the yellow cat at the door, she flings herself toward it, hissing and slapping the glass with her paws. The yellow cat, which is about two or three times Hendry's size, simply looks perplexed by all the fuss.

On one occasion the door was open when Hendry charged. I think it surprised both Hendry and the yellow cat. The yellow cat backed away a step or two. Having made her point, Hendry flounced back into the house.

I've never seen the two cats actually fight; often they curl up within a couple of feet of each other.

On my desk is a list of Rules for Dealing with Stray Cats that a friend gave my wife.

Rule 1 states that "Stray cats will not be fed."

I've obviously violated that one, as well as Rule 5 (stray cats will not be encouraged to make this house their permanent residence).

I have honored Rule 2 (stray cats will not be fed anything except dry cat food) and the part of Rule 7 that says stray cats "will absolutely not be given a name."

Hendry—who is curled up by my keyboard as I write—is drawing the line at Rule 8: stray cats with or without a name will not be allowed inside the house.

The yellow cat seems willing to accept that as long as I keep putting the food dish out.

What Is Really Important

September 2003

AN ACQUAINTANCE AND I compared notes not long ago about events that forced us to take a fresh look at our lives.

He had recently survived a heart attack. There was nothing in his appearance (he's slim and fit), family history or medical examinations to warn that he was a candidate. His physician said that if he had not been in such good physical condition, he probably would have died.

The attack came suddenly, without warning.

It has been a little more than four years since an angry looking mole appeared on my back. It turned out to be a melanoma. Like my acquaintance, I was fortunate. The cancer had not spread. Even so, I still have periodic visits with the doctor to check for a recurrence.

My acquaintance and I are like many others who have come face to face with their own mortality. The experience left us with changed perspectives and different ideas on how we should spend the time that we more fully realize is a gift.

I wonder whether these brushes with mortality hasten a process that is already at work in many people. It had always been a puzzle to me why older people, who presumably have fewer years left on earth, often display more patience than those who are younger. Perhaps years, like life-threatening situations, encourage a greater examination of what is truly important.

I don't know how it will be with my acquaintance; his experience is more recent than mine.

It will be, I suspect, rather like my own. After a while, it becomes easy to forget how crystal clear our values became. I sometimes find that I am getting angry over matters that are of no lasting importance or I am beginning to obsess over the trivial, things I have said I would not do.

I have to remind myself of those decisions I made about what was important and how I would spend my energies and worries. Thus far I have been able to remember clearly the days when I was making those judgments.

In the past week or so, we have all gotten a more removed lesson in mortality and in what is important. We have seen how in a matter of hours some lives can be lost and others changed in ways they might never have suspected.

Most of us, I suspect, spent more time than usual last week with the television on, mesmerized by the force of Hurricane Katrina. The suffering we have seen has made our problems seem so small.

We have told ourselves to complain no more about such things as the electricity going out or about the price of a gallon of gasoline.

We meant it when we said it, but in time the events that triggered our vows become more remote, and we become again what we were.

To a large degree, that is to be expected.

It might be enlightening, though, to stop occasionally and recall what we thought was important in the immediate aftermath of the disaster.

Disconnecting? Just Recharging

April 2003

THERE ARE A COUPLE of Adirondack chairs on our front deck that invite you to linger. Once you've sat back for a while, you can think of all sorts of reasons to sit for another few minutes.

They don't get used nearly enough.

But this is that marvelous time of the year when the air is soft and the evenings demand appreciation.

We migrated to the deck one recent evening to sit for a spell before starting dinner. There were no lights on inside the house, no television reporting relentlessly on the crisis of the moment.

The sky beyond the Smith Mountain fire tower was still aglow, the color of the dying embers of a charcoal fire. The fishermen had gone home, and the water was as flat as an artist's canvas.

Evening gathered, and the outdoor lights twinkled on at the houses around the slough, their reflections painting straight lines in the water aimed right at us.

Gradually stars appeared, at first the few bright ones, then a sky full of stars. The lights of Alexander City glow on the horizon, not enough to blot out the dark sky.

All around, fireflies flashed their silent signals, more than I can ever recall seeing at one time.

Our conversation was punctuated with long silences as all of our senses soaked up the spring evening.

It took a while for me to realize what I was not hearing: no whining of heat pumps or air conditioning units, no roar of lawn mowers or weed trimmers, not even the sounds of faraway traffic.

No human voices, no music blaring from outdoor speakers.

Somewhere down the way a dog saw or heard something, or thought it did, and soon all of the dogs were passing the word along the canine version of the jungle telegraph.

They settled down eventually, and we heard only the insects and tree frogs that provide the evening's sound track.

The gaps in the conversation grew longer.

I thought about a newspaper report I saw recently on a study of the health costs of the American trend toward skipping vacations.

In a nine-year study of middle-age men who were at risk for coronary disease, researchers found that those who didn't take vacations were more likely to die, particularly from heart disease, than men who took regular vacations. A study published a decade ago found that a lack of vacations was a predictor of heart attacks and early deaths among women.

That's just a couple of more stones in a wall of evidence that 24/7 may be okay for some machines, but not necessarily for people.

Despite that, as corporate America tries to do more work with fewer employees, many people just don't feel that they can take time off. Some worry that leaving the office for a couple of weeks sends a signal that they're not essential. Those who do, nominally, take time often use laptop computers, cell phones and wireless personal digital assistants to remain plugged into work.

That, says one of the authors of the study, can create a condition that simply magnifies stress.

The news story quoted one physician who's found that even short breaks from work can relieve symptoms of stress.

The secret is not just to get away physically, but to get away mentally.

I've found that an hour or so in an Adirondack chair, listening to the quiet and gazing into the depths of the universe does wonders.

It's not so much being disconnected as it is recharging.

Age of Disappearing Information

June 2003

WE LIVE IN AN age of instant information, but we also are living in an age of disappearing information.

That was brought home in an article I read the other day—in an online magazine of all places. It contended that e-mail is wrecking our national archives. It's an issue that should cause some concern; more than national archives are at stake. Just as troubling is the disappearance of information about the lives of ordinary people before their descendants have an opportunity to know what they were like.

On the issue of official information, Fred Kaplan, writing in Slate, said that the widespread use of e-mail will rob historians writing about the most recent Gulf War (and the first Gulf War and the war over Kosovo) of the trove of documents that have allowed them to examine how decisions were made in earlier eras.

Certain high-level documents are usually kept, Kaplan said, but "beneath that level, it's hit and miss, more often miss."

It may be easier to persuade the government to save more documents than it will be to find ways to preserve the chronicles of everyday life that tell us who we are and where we came from.

So much of what we know about the lives of our own forebears

—their tragedies and their triumphs, the mundane details of everyday life—comes from letters. They have provided a feast for historians and for professional and amateur genealogists.

It wasn't the official records of John Adams' long public service that allowed historian David McCullough to write such a compelling biography of the second president. It was because Adams and his wife, Abigail, were such prolific correspondents. Their letters, McCullough wrote, "number in the thousands, and because they both wrote with such consistent candor and in such vivid detail, it is possible to know them—to go beneath the surface of their lives ...."

In Ken Burns' epic history of the American Civil War, the most poignant moments came when the narrators read vivid, heart-felt letters from the battle field and from the home front.

All across the country threads of our collective history are tucked away in nooks and crannies: Love letters wrapped in ribbon in the back of a dresser drawer; a shoebox on a closet shelf with letters home from a young man half a world away in the frozen mountains of Korea or the steaming jungles of Vietnam.

But, I fear, the age of the personal letter is passing, perhaps has passed.

Who writes letters anymore? Sitting down with pen and paper takes time; composing a thoughtful letter requires thought. Even the mechanical skill of writing seems to be fading; a newspaper article recently discussed the difficulty of getting children to learn cursive writing when they already are comfortable with computer keyboards. In some places, cursive writing is no longer a required subject; it probably isn't even an elective.

Even folks who grew up in the age of fountain pens and bond writing paper have computers now, and it's much easier to dash off an e-mail in the abbreviated style of the electronic age. The absence of complete sentences or even complete thoughts is hardly noted.

Although e-mail has had a part in the decline of personal correspondence, I think it started long before the Internet. Blame lower long distance rates.

I grew up in an age in which long distance telephone calls were reserved for matters that were timely and important. For anything else, a letter filled the bill.

My children think nothing of picking up the phone to call a friend on the other side of the country just to chat.

Today's communication is instantaneous—and evanescent. Does anyone print out a love e-mail (if there is such a thing) and save it to read in the future? Does anyone make and keep notes about telephone conversations with family members?

I remember the tingle of pleasure I got as a grade-schooler when I received a letter from my pen pal in Australia. There's still pleasure in finding a personal letter among all the bills and sales material that fill the mailbox.

I confess, though, that I have joined the rest of the world in relying on e-mail and the telephone.

Perhaps we can do our descendants—and future historians—a favor if we occasionally turn off the computer, put down the telephone, and take pen in hand.

Tiny Chigger, Big Itch

June 2003

FOR CAUSING PURE, unadulterated misery, there are few things worse than chigger bites. I use the plural, because I rarely get just one bite.

The facts that the chiggers found in the United States aren't known to carry any diseases and that attaching itself to a human being is a fatal mistake on the chigger's part are of little comfort.

They certainly weren't much comfort the other night as I sought something to ease the itching so I could get some sleep. In a way, the itching was my own fault. I had almost finished running the string trimmer when I realized that I hadn't sprayed myself with insect repellent. Although repellent isn't 100 percent effective, it does help. I knew I would pay a price for my oversight.

Our half hill isn't really landscaped. Wild azaleas and hydrangeas grow among the trees, and much of the ground is covered with fallen leaves. All of that makes for easy maintenance, but it also creates a resort for chiggers.

Of course, you can't easily tell where chiggers are lurking. Some spots are infested with islands of chiggers; other, similar spots don't have a single one. Many of us learned as children that chiggers—or red bugs as we in the South call them—are common around blackberry bushes.

Regardless of where they are, chiggers aren't lying in wait just to make our lives miserable, says Gary Mullen, a professor of entomology at Auburn University. Their preferred host, he said, is much smaller, such as a lizard or a rodent.

Chiggers can be found on wild turkeys, birds, even frogs, Mullen said. In fact, thousands of chiggers were counted on a single black snake, which was not showing any signs of distress.

They can be found throughout the United States, Mullen said. I suspect we're more aware of them in the South because we have more warm months when both we and the chiggers are active.

If you have good vision and look closely when you first feel an itch, before you start scratching, you may see a tiny, orange looking dot. You definitely can see one with a low-power magnifying glass. I've never seen one; I guess I've always scratched before I looked.

If you could see one really well, you would see a hairy little six-legged creature about 1/150th to 1/120th of an inch in diameter.

The creature you would see is not an insect but the larval stage of a kind of mite that is a distant relative to spiders.

After it hatched from an egg, the chigger climbed up onto a grass stem, a leaf or some other vegetation and waited. If you brushed by before some other host did, the chigger crawled aboard. It then found a protected place—a fold in the skin like the back of your knee or your armpit, or a place where the clothing fit tight, like your waistband—and went to work.

A chigger bite may feel a mile deep, but it isn't. The chigger doesn't burrow into the skin; it finds an opening in the skin, like a hair follicle, and injects a salivary secretion containing a digestive enzyme that breaks down skin cells into a liquid the chigger can ingest. The digestive fluid causes the surrounding tissue to become inflamed. Your skin reacts by turning red and starting to itch.

The itch seems to magnify when you are trying to sleep.

Ointments made with benzocaine and hydrocortisone offer some relief, as does calamine lotion. Some people swear by meat tenderizer, a dab of kerosene or even a coat of clear fingernail polish over the bite. Someone told me the other day that Preparation H helps.

I've never found anything that takes away the itch for very long.

Mullen said that when they feed on the right host, chiggers engorge themselves and drop off. They become eight-legged nymphs and then adult mites. The nymphs and adults eat tiny eggs, including mosquito eggs.

When they latch onto a human, though, the chiggers are sealing their own fate, Mullen said. Chiggers aren't very good guests, and people aren't very good hosts.

Mullen once used his own ankle as a chigger lab. He circled 70 chigger bites and he and his colleagues kept track of what happened. Within 24 hours, 75 percent of the chiggers had died. Within 48 hours, 96 percent of them had died.

The chiggers that were making me miserable the other night died, too. I'd have been just as happy if they'd found a more amenable host.

(Legal) Mood Enhancer

July 2003

I FELT UNUSUALLY energetic the other morning when I set out on my walk. At first I couldn't figure out why; then I realized that I was looking at blue sky, acres of blue sky. There were some clouds, but they were the puffy cumulus variety that is typical of this time of year. The air, for a change, didn't feel as if I could wring water out of it with my bare hands.

Veteran outdoors people refer to a patch of blue in an otherwise cloudy sky as a sucker hole. Sucker holes are like the sirens in Greek mythology. They lure people into danger. Sailors see a sucker hole and take small boats onto big water, convinced the weather's improving. Non-instrument-rated pilots take off because they think they can climb atop the clouds through the sucker hole.

We've had sucker holes lately, but this wasn't one of them.

Still, I haven't been complaining—at least not aloud. During the time that we hopefully searched the sky for clouds that might contain rain, I promised, perhaps rashly, that if rain ever returned, I would not complain.

I hadn't realized, though, how much the weather had affected my mood.

73

Experts say that our memory is heavily influenced by recent events, and it certainly seems that it has been months since everything dried out.

Mildew—always present when you build among the trees—has thrived like never before on our siding and soffits. Even parts of the house that I've scrubbed between showers look as if they've never been touched. Several weeks ago, I made the mistake of opening the screen doors that lead onto our front deck; they have swollen so much that they're impossible to close. It'll take a long dry spell before they will close easily.

We've never had much of a mosquito problem before this year. Puddles that used to dry up in a day now linger long enough for mosquito eggs to hatch, and my ankles serve as a moving buffet when I go out to the road to pick up the morning paper.

The cane that I am trying to eradicate—there doesn't seem to be any effective way to get rid of it except to dig it out—is getting ahead of me again while it is too muddy to dig.

It has taken a certain amount of resolve of late just to go for a walk. It's almost diabolical the way the skies wait to open up until I am at the far point of my route. It hasn't really mattered, though. Even if it hasn't rained, there's been so much moisture in the air that I have been soaked anyway.

The grass along the roadside produces seed heads before the county can mow it. The tall grass conceals the litter, but when traffic forces me to walk on the shoulder, I emerge with tiny black seeds sticking to my socks and skin.

Even on the days when there has been blue sky—sucker holes? —the air has been heavy and clouds have gathered and thunder has rattled the china. The sky was clear the other day when I opened the patio umbrella to rid it of the mildew it had been gathering while it sat closed. I left it open to dry.

The aluminum umbrella pole goes through a hole in the patio table and anchors in a heavy base.

In the afternoon, in the space of only a few minutes, the angry clouds boiled up, and the trees began swaying nervously.

From the kitchen, I could see the edges of the umbrella trembling.

Before I could race to close it, the wind scooped the umbrella up —along with the table and the base—tilted it sideways and launched it like a missile over the deck railing. It fetched up against a tree about 30 feet away. After the rain stopped, we went to retrieve it. The aluminum pole and several of the ribs were bent, but they were easily straightened. The only damage to the table was some dirt.

As my son the optimist would have pointed out, we were lucky that the wind didn't aim the umbrella and table toward the glass windows or doors.

When I got home from my walk, I looked at the weather forecast for the rest of the week. Only the afternoon and evening thunderstorms that are common for this time of year were in the outlook for the rest of week. The little symbol for the weekend weather, though, was another dark cloud.

The day will come when we wish desperately for rain, so I won't complain. And I'll regard every patch of blue sky—sucker hole or not—as a legal mood enhancer.

August Made Good Memories

July 2003

AUGUST. ENDLESS DAYS with no breath of coolness in the breeze. Nights spent turning the pillow over and over, searching for a cool spot. For a school kid in a bygone era, August was when summer vacation began to be boring.

That's something most Alabama school kids don't have to worry about. Some of them are back in school already; others will be soon. Football players are working to get in shape and musicians are attending band camp.

It seems that young people benefit from today's school calendar, but they're missing something, too.

We didn't believe it when the grownups talked about how time flies. By August the clock moved as slowly as a dog searching for a spot of shade. By August we had tired of most summer activities.

We had filled our pockets with blackberries and suffered the agonies of the bites of the red bugs that we had collected with them. No home remedy worked for long. We had splashed in the creek and fished in the pond with worms we'd dug in the chicken yard.

Nobody's house had air conditioning. Television hadn't arrived yet. Movies—in a cool, dark theater—were a Saturday afternoon treat.

Fortunately, there were usually enough of us around to collaborate in inventing things to combat the boredom of August. It was the month that we seemed to do more things to get ourselves in trouble.

"You boys" was a collective heard often in August, usually preceding a lecture by someone's grandfather.

On a farm, there are many opportunities for the active mind.

Our cousin's grandfather was a cabinet maker who had a fine collection of tools, which our cousin felt free to borrow without asking. Sometimes those tools found their way deep into the woods. Often they stayed there.

"You boys must think tools grow out of the ground," my cousin's grandfather would growl. "You've got them planted all over the woods."

Sometimes he got annoyed enough to cuss. He could cuss better than anybody we knew, and it was a part of our education to hear him. But his anger blew over fairly quickly.

Lumber abounds on a farm, too, and it also ended up in the woods. It went into the construction of forts and tree houses—platforms really—that would have scared our parents silly if they'd seen them. It's one of life's miracles that none of those platforms sent us plunging to death or disfigurement.

Perhaps our closest brush with real trouble, though, came close to home—in the hay barn.

Every summer, the barn's loft was stacked to the rafters with freshly baled hay. It was a great place to play hide and seek, and nobody complained about us mangling a few bales. The most fun, though, was to climb up stacks of bales to the cupola which sat atop the roof like a little house with louvered sides. It was a wonderful aerie from which to spy on the world. All it lacked for real comfort was a floor. So we appropriated lumber and tools and installed one, careful to time our project for when my grandfather wasn't around.

We hadn't yet learned about the heat that green hay generates and the need to let that hot air escape.

Several days passed before my grandfather learned of our little construction project.

He was about as upset as I had ever seen him—and we had done lots of things that didn't quite meet his approval.

"You kids (as I recall, my sister was involved in that misadventure)," he said, "are going to burn the barn down."

Our only punishment, though, was to rip out the floor that we were so proud of. Even that episode could be counted as educational. We now knew about spontaneous combustion in a way that we would never have learned in school.

In thinking about those long ago Augusts, I am reminded of an episode from Calvin and Hobbes—perhaps the best comic strip there ever was.

In it, Calvin is at the window telling his tiger friend Hobbes that in the short term it would make him happy to go play outside. In the long term, he says, it would make him happier to do well at school and become successful. The third panel shows the two of them zipping down the hill on a sled, and Calvin is saying, "But in the very long term, I know which will make better memories."

August made some pretty good memories.

Sometimes Listening Is Enough

August 2003

THE SCENE PLAYED out as it so often does: Strangers are thrown together by circumstance. Someone breaks the ice, and they find that they have more in common than they might have thought. Confidences are shared; often it's easier to share personal information with someone you'll probably never see again than with closer acquaintances.

Many of us have sat next to someone on an airplane or a bus and learned far more about that person than we know about some of our coworkers.

The venue this time, though, was the customer lounge of an automobile dealership. Three people—an older white woman, a younger black woman, and a man in his 60s—all of them, as it turned out, from different communities. All were waiting for their vehicles to be serviced.

There always has to be someone to initiate conversation among strangers, but the others have to accept the invitation.

This conversation was initiated by the older woman. She offered a comment about Gov. Bob Riley's tax and reform package.

There was only a short silence before the others joined in with their opinions. Somehow the talk about tax reform turned to the

New Testament's injunction about feeding the hungry, taking in strangers, and visiting the sick and those in prison.

Eventually, the retired teacher, herself a picture of propriety, disclosed—almost shyly—that she had a brother in prison. "Drugs," she explained.

Some of the family members had disowned him, she said, but she thought it was her duty to continue to love him and to visit him.

The other woman nodded sympathetically. She, too, had a brother who had been seduced by drugs. He had done his time, but he had lasted only a few days in rehab. He wasn't stealing from the family—she made sure of that.

We all know that drugs have infiltrated communities large and small, but the women seemed to find comfort in talking with someone who knew their feelings.

Then the younger woman's car was ready, and she left.

The conversation however, went on, darting from topic to topic without any apparent road map, its direction dictated by the woman.

The woman had been widowed early in her married life and had never remarried. After spending a career teaching in a metropolitan area she had returned to the small community of her roots to nurse a dying mother.

Although she talked about many friends and relatives, the woman seemed to have saved up a store of things that she needed to put in words, and she rushed along as if she feared she would run out of time.

Amid all the bits of self-disclosure, the man realized, a thread had emerged. The woman seemed to have spent a lifetime thinking more about what would make other people happy than about what was important to her.

Now she had some decisions to make about her own life. She wasn't looking for answers; talking seemed to be sufficient.

The book that the man had brought to read while his car was being serviced lay unopened on the chair next to him. It could wait.

Sometimes taking in strangers just means taking time to listen.

One Thing at a Time

September 2003

I AM TRYING to learn a new skill, or rather trying to re-learn an old one: unitasking, (or, perhaps, monotasking). I must confess that I'm finding it a challenge.

Unitasking doesn't appear in my Oxford American Dictionary, but it ought to. It's the opposite of multitasking, a word that does appear in that tome.

Although the dictionary is relatively new, it defines multitasking in its original sense: the simultaneous execution of more than one program or task by a single computer processor.

We know that's only part of the definition. We humans were multitasking long before the word was invented.

Multitasking has become a buzzword in a downsized economy as fewer employees are asked to do more and more jobs.

We're learning that multitasking isn't as big a boon to productivity as it sounds. Several recent studies have found that efficiency actually goes down as the number of tasks being juggled increases. A study published in a psychology journal a couple of years ago found that as chores become more complex the "time cost" of switching from one task to another becomes greater.

At its worst, multitasking isn't just inefficient; it's downright dangerous. The use of cell phones in busy traffic is a favorite example, but certainly not the only one. According to the National Highway Traffic Safety Administration, 25 percent of all car crashes are related to distractions.

I learned long ago that a career in journalism seems to shorten the attention span so that it spoils you for any other line of work. I realize now that multitasking was at least part of that. Working on many different tasks at the same time is a part of the game.

Juggling a multitude of interesting things at one time can be exhilarating, but when you get too many balls in the air, it's easy to drop some of them.

How many times have you suddenly realized that the person with whom you are talking has asked a question and is waiting for a response? But you don't have any idea what the question was because you were thinking of the telephone call you need to make, the letter you need to write or the meeting coming up in a few minutes.

How many times has your spouse asked you about something that you discussed an hour or a day earlier? How many times has your spouse believed that the discussion never took place?

Perhaps these aren't so much cases of wandering minds as of too much multitasking.

There's no need to eliminate multitasking altogether. Not all tasks require our full attention. Raking the leaves or taking a walk, often frees the mind to consider other matters. Most of what passes for entertainment on television probably is better if you don't give it your full attention.

But I am trying to limit the number of balls I have in the air at one time. I found that I do my least satisfactory—and least satisfying—work when I'm trying to do, or think about, too many things at one time.

Children are perhaps the best teachers of unitasking. Have you ever noticed how totally absorbed a child can be in whatever he or she is doing at the moment, whether it's reading a book or playing a game.

We seem, however, to be turning our children into little multitaskers. Nowadays kids seem to have as many demands as adults do, and it's a little sad to realize that planning calendars and personal digital assistants are among the must-have items for the back to school set.

I wonder whether we might eventually lose the ability to focus our concentration on a single matter.

Meanwhile, I'm trying to identify more of those things that deserve full attention, whether it's really listening to a grandchild or appreciating the magic of a sunset.

Blue Skies There All Along

November 2003

THE QUESTION FROM my brother—and his own answer to the question a week or so later—was a reminder of something that I already know but too often fail to heed.

We were having one of our regular telephone chats a couple of months ago when my brother, who lives in North Louisiana where we grew up, had a question. "Why aren't there blue skies like there were when we were kids? Has the air pollution gotten that bad?"

It seemed to him, he said, that he hadn't seen those clean blue skies and puffy white clouds that had been a fixture of our boyhood summers.

Although we had a rainy summer at the lake, the skies on the clear days had seemed to me to be as blue as ever, but I told myself I would look further.

The next time we talked, though, my brother had found his own answer.

He had driven over to East Texas on business, he said, and the sky was so blue that it stretched into infinity, and the cumulus clouds were as light as cotton candy.

"The good Lord hit me upside the head and told me I hadn't been looking," he said.

My brother works hard, and he gets absorbed in what he's doing. He is not different from many of us in that regard. We get so busy with everyday demands that we tune out the world around us.

It is as if we wait until we take a vacation to turn our senses on.

We go to the beach and breathe deeply, savoring the smell of salt in the air. We listen to the sigh of the waves as they embrace the beach and then pull away. Our taste buds are attuned to every subtlety of the food before us.

We retreat to the mountains and luxuriate in the softness of the air. We are hypnotized by the play of light and shadows as the sun climbs over the ridge line and then disappears behind another one.

In a village we find charm in an old building. In a city we feel the energy.

We appreciate the flowers by the roadside and the grace of a horse running free through a pasture.

It is as if we are truly alive and we have discovered that the world is full of wonders.

And then we return home, settle into our routine and turn our senses off.

It is a challenge to do otherwise. The chore list is always too long and the day is too short. For most of us, that is just the way life is. I am fortunate enough to have more control over my time than I have had since early childhood, but I still find that my days brim with things that I have to do and things I think I have to do.

Even in our busiest days, though, it is possible to take a moment to realize that we don't have to travel far from home to find some of the world's wonder.

On one recent morning, my wife and I were on our walk. The road stretched down a long hill that ended in the lake. The sun was rising somewhere behind us, illuminating the trees that line the road. In the distance, the early morning mist rose off the water and climbed above the trees at the bottom of the hill. Beyond the mist was another ridge line. The trees there were almost silhouettes.

A hazard warning light blinked on a radio tower on a more distant ridge. A pileated woodpecker flew overhead, its complaining cry fracturing the stillness.

Fifteen or 20 minutes later, it was full daylight, and there was a long list of things to do.

But those few minutes were a small vacation, and a reminder that there are wonders around us.

My brother says that he's going to be more aware of such things.

Maybe all of us could benefit by a lick upside the head and an admonition that we're not paying enough attention.

Well Fed Assassins?

December 2003

IN THE EARLY MORNING quiet as I have my cereal and orange juice, life teems just outside the dining room window.

A pileated woodpecker is drilling in a dead tree limb. A crow lights on a pine bough, apparently waiting to see what direction his friends are going. Soon it flies off in the company of several others. I'm just as glad that they're taking their coarse chorus elsewhere.

One of the family of squirrels that lives on our half hill races up and down the trees, jumping from one pencil-thin limb to another. The squirrels appear graceful, but I've witnessed more than one misstep. Once a squirrel plummeted onto our front deck. I caught the last part of the fall from the corner of my eye and heard the impact.

When I went out to investigate, the squirrel was lying very still. I feared that it was dead, but in a few moments the squirrel began to twitch a little, like a boxer regaining consciousness after a knockout.

I went inside and watched as the squirrel crawled gingerly around the deck. Soon it hopped onto the railing. Within minutes, the squirrel raced up the porch screening, leapt to a limb and disappeared into the heights of a tree.

On this morning, the squirrel seems to be gathering acorns, which have been abundant this year.

The squirrel (I suspect that only one of them is my true adversary) and I seem to have reached a standoff regarding the bird feeder, which hangs from a limb just outside the dining room window. The squirrel managed to loot several previous feeders, even carrying one whole feeder away entirely.

This latest feeder is more challenging. With a long pole, I managed to pass a piece of clothes line wire over a tree limb. Attached to the wire is a small pulley with a thin nylon cord threaded through it. I attached the wire to a hook on the tree trunk so that the pulley hangs just below the limb. The feeder is attached to the end of the cord and hangs about four feet below the limb. The cord allows me to lower the feeder to the ground to refill it.

It has a shutter mechanism, so that even if the squirrel managed to cling to it, the food supply would be inaccessible.

When the feeder first went up, the squirrel spent hours reconnoitering. The cord is too thin to climb down, and the feeder is so high off the ground that the possibility of missing makes the risk of jumping onto it unappealing, even to a daredevil squirrel.

I don't fool myself that the ceasefire is permanent. Sooner or later the squirrel will figure out that it can chew through the wire or the cord and send the feeder crashing to the ground where it can be robbed at leisure.

Meanwhile, birds flit through the trees nearby. They dart to the feeder in ones and twos, grab a few bites, and go to the end of the line. Purple finches, tufted titmice and chickadees predominate at the moment. Doves wait on the ground below, grateful for the table scraps.

As I watch, a red-bellied woodpecker makes several trips to the feeder, dining at leisure. If a smaller bird approaches, the woodpecker dispatches it with a threatening shake of its head.

It is perhaps indicative of the welfare state I am running that the birds gather even if the feeder is empty, confident of a refill.

The cats, whose dishes are nearly always full, are members of the welfare class, too, and show no interest in the birds.

I don't think Hendry, the mostly indoor cat, or Yellow Cat, the outdoor cat, would take a swipe at a bird if it paraded on the ground in front of them. It's difficult to remember that a little more than a year ago Yellow Cat was skinny and living by his wits, running away if a human came anywhere near.

I have read, though, that cats—feral and well fed domestics—kill 4 to 5 million birds a day in the United States.

Perhaps Hendry and Yellow Car really are assassins. If so, they hide their profession as successfully as a Mafia hit-man residing quietly in the suburbs, and both the birds and I are taken in.

The Best Christmas Gift

December 2003

CHRISTMAS MORNING at our house will be quiet.

With no house guests for this holiday, we will get to sleep in—at least as late as we can sleep anymore. We are finding, with some regret, that there is truth in the observation that as you get older you sleep less.

In Montgomery, our three granddaughters, I am sure, will awaken early, and the house will be filled with excitement and strewn with wrapping paper.

Several time zones away, our grandson has been anticipating Christmas for weeks. This is the first year that he has been old enough to really tune into the season. At five months, his younger sister doesn't know what the hubbub is all about.

I am not dismayed at the prospect of a quiet morning. We had our years of trying to keep the kids in bed at least until daybreak and watching their excitement as they opened gifts.

Now it's our children's turn to share the excitement with their children. As much as we like to have the children at our house, we understand that children can better celebrate Christmas at home.

We will catch up with the Montgomery branch of the family at a more civilized time, and e-mail and telephones will allow us to share the holiday with the Arizona children.

Christmas at our house will almost be an anticlimax.

For a week or so, our living room would have given an OSHA inspector the shudders. Boxes, bags, sacks, rolls of wrapping papers, ribbons, bows, scissors and tape covered the floor, the couch, the coffee table, even the easy chair.

Fortunately, they all were boxed up and entrusted to the package delivery folks before I tripped over something and broke either my neck or a present.

Packages have begun arriving, too, but they're already wrapped and can be placed neatly under the tree.

I did not have much of a role in generating the pile of presents that spilled over our living room. I don't have a philosophical objection to shopping, but it is not something I particularly enjoy. When I go to a store, it is usually because I already know what I am after. I find it, pay for it, and leave. It is only in hardware stores and book stores that I can wander the aisles and find things I didn't even know I wanted or needed.

My shopping this Christmas season has been largely limited to waiting patiently and carrying parcels. I was even spared some of that, because my wife has adopted online shopping for gifts that aren't easily available locally. Many of those gifts go straight from merchant to recipient without even passing through our cluttered living room.

There's little wonder that revenue starved state governments are hungrily eyeing internet commerce. If my wife, who is hardly an early adopter of technology, is spending significant dollars online, you can be sure that there are big bucks flowing out there, just waiting to be taxed.

I have heard some people complain that they get Christmas wish lists that are so specific as to model number, color, etc., that they might was well be requisitions or purchase orders. That's the kind of thing that would encourage online shopping since there's no joy of discovering just the right thing for someone, something that will be a delightful surprise.

Fortunately, we don't get those kinds of requests, although parents and grandparents do coordinate on gifts for the young ones so there's no duplication. The little kids are surprised and delighted no matter what they get.

No doubt we will find surprises and delights under our tree, and we will be grateful.

But what might be the most delightful presents—the ones we give to each other—won't be under the tree.

Neither of us could think of things that we wanted. What we really wanted was time, time to enjoy what we already have, time to enjoy this world that we live in. So our gift to each other is the promise that we will make, take or steal that most elusive of gifts—time that is our own.

Honesty Only Skin Deep?

January 2004

HANGING AROUND THE college newspaper office years ago, we occasionally amused ourselves by combining parts of clichés with parts of other clichés to create new expressions that could become clichés on their own..

Among those we came up with were "beauty is the best policy" and "honesty is only skin deep."

It is the latter expression that has come to mind more than once in recent months as I have listened to business owners talk with frustration about the difficulty of finding honest employees.

Since those business owners are actively trying to deal with theft problems, I won't use their names.

Anyway, I am sure they are representative of many other employers. The U.S. Department of Commerce estimates that 30 percent of business failures result from employee theft.

I cannot say with certainty that dishonesty is more widespread than it once was. Every generation seems to see moral decline in the generation that comes behind it. I do sense, however, that there are fewer qualms about cheating and stealing.

Cheating on tests and submitting papers copied off the Internet as one's own work are more widely regarded by students as acceptable. So is downloading movies and music without paying for them. With that mindset, helping oneself to the employer's money or property would hardly seem any different.

One business owner I know said plaintively, "We know we have people stealing, but we're reluctant to fire them for fear their replacements might steal more."

Based on figures cited by the Small Business Administration, he might be right. The SBA quoted security experts as saying that as many as 30 percent of all employees do steal and that another 60 percent will steal if given sufficient motive and opportunity.

The other businessman I talked with about the problem recently has grown what started as a sideline into a thriving enterprise. He did it by working 12-14 hours a day, seven days a week.

Growth meant that he couldn't do it all himself. He pays better than the prevailing wages, but more than once he has found that people in whom he had placed trust were thieves, even ones who had the ability and energy to move up in the business..

"If I ever decide to close or sell, it will be because of dishonest employees," he said.

In looking over material about employee dishonesty, I find all kinds of explanations why people steal. They steal because they think they're being underpaid. They steal because they think they're treated unfairly. They steal because they have debts. And many of them steal because they have drug habits.

They steal because they don't think what they take will really hurt the business.

Mostly, I suspect, they steal because they can.

"I just made it too easy for them to steal," said one of the business owners.

He is changing many procedures and is investing a significant amount of money in equipment to help detect theft.

His attempts to make it more difficult to steal square with what the experts recommend.

But those responses, as sensible as they are, don't really come to grips with the larger question: What happened to the notion that taking things that belong to other people is wrong?

The businessmen's responsibility is to deal with the world that is. We all have some responsibility for attaining the world that ought to be.

I can't help wondering about the future of a society that has accepted the notion that honesty is only skin deep.

Good Old Days? Maybe

January 2004

AMONG MY MEMENTOES is an old Gillette safety razor. I am glad to have it; it stirs pleasant memories. I am equally glad that I do not have to shave with it.

The old razor consists of three parts: a slightly curved cap with a threaded extension, a base, and a handle. A double-edged razor blade was placed between the cap and the base, and whole affair screwed into the handle. The razor was brass-plated, but some of the plating wore off in years of use, exposing the shiny silver metal beneath.

That old razor has lasted a lot longer than any of the razors I have used in recent years.

It is a tangible reminder of one of my forebears.

It is also a reminder that the Good Old Days were not as good as we sometimes remember. The old razor—more accurately, the blades used with it—couldn't give as smooth a shave as present day razors, and styptic pencils were as necessary as shaving lather. Those of us who had experience scraping our skin with blades that were dull before even one shave was finished regard the introduction of stainless steel blades as one of the great advances of civilization. And things have only gotten better from there.

Although elders of the tribe seem to enjoy talking about the past, usually nostalgically, memory is selective. Of course, we are not alone in doing that. Now that they are in their 30s and have children of their own, our sons indulge in their own memory stirring.

The big difference is that the more time we've had, the more memories we've amassed. And, as writer Franklin P. Adams observed, nothing is more responsible for the Good Old Days than a bad memory.

Objectively, there's a lot about the Good Old Days that can't hold a candle to the present.

My heart still goes thump-thump when I see a 1957 Chevrolet convertible. But that Chevy would have been worn out long before it reached the 100,000 plus miles that are on my wife's Toyota. And we still think of the latter automobile as relatively new.

Somewhere in the attic, I think, there is an old upright typewriter. It weighs about as much as a boat anchor, and typing on it qualifies as manual labor.

The typewriter, whose design was not much changed from decades earlier, is a lot sturdier than the keyboard and the printer that are attached to my computer. In terms of real dollars, the typewriter was far more expensive than both of those items together. And when they wear out, it will be cheaper to replace them with something that is even better than it would be to repair them, if repairs were even possible.

My friends who play golf assure me that golf clubs and balls are much more forgiving than they were when I last played 30 odd years ago. I hope to put their word to the test soon if I don't do something ill advised with my back first.

Illnesses or injuries that would have condemned us to long periods of misery or even death in years past are treated routinely now, sometimes on an outpatient basis.

I'd much rather have a bum ticker or a bum knee now than in the 1960s or '70s.

If you made a list of things that are better and put it alongside a list of things that are more flimsily made, I'm confident that the list of improvements would be longer.

I am not confident, though, that having better things has left us better off.

It seems to me that overall we are more tense and uncertain than we were even in the era in which the United States and the Soviet Union stared at each other across the nuclear divide.

We seem to have less confidence that life can be better for all members of society and that it is worthwhile to try to make it so.

Several years ago Robert D. Putnam wrote a book called "Bowling Alone: The Collapse and Revival of American Community."

The author used extensive data to show that Americans are increasingly disconnected from family, friends and our democratic structures.

He says that America has reinvented itself before and that it can do so again.

I hope he's right.

While we're doing it, I'll be glad to hang onto all those things that work better than they did in the Good Old Days.

Destination Optional

February 2004

I WENT FOR A ride the other day. Not a planned trip, but an aimless meander with no specific destination and no deadline for getting there.

I did it simply because nobody seems to go for a ride anymore except teen-agers, and their rides follow familiar routes so they can see and be seen—and I wanted to see whether it was still fun.

There are two kinds of rides.

On one kind you set out deliberately, perhaps with some general idea of where you are going. The other is a spontaneous exploration. You are driving along—most likely on the way to somewhere—and you say to yourself, I wonder where that road goes? So you turn and find out.

At one time, a Sunday afternoon drive was a standard form of recreation. The family would pile into the car and head out to see some of the world around them. Often the drive would include a stop to visit with friends.

In the country, farmers liked to take a Sunday afternoon drive to see how others' crops were doing.

99

When my grandfather decided he could no longer drive safely, he recruited one of the kids to chauffeur him in his old Studebaker truck. He liked to ride out to a spot overlooking the construction work on the Interstate highway. The boredom for the kids was balanced by getting a chance to drive. Usually there was a soda pop to be had, too.

Those drives—or rides, if you prefer—were before the days of television and air conditioning, before all of our minutes, even our recreation time, were programmed and organized. Now we are always on our way to somewhere. We are scheduled and committed, and we go down strange roads only if we miss a turn on our way to our destination.

All of that came to mind the other night when I pulled out a road map to plan a trip. I realized that there were so many roads around home that I had never driven on.

So one recent day, despite the fact that I had things I could do, should do, I set out to explore those roads.

The rain had moved out and the wind was busy chasing away the clouds to reveal a washed out blue sky.

I had my Tallapoosa County road map with me. I didn't use it so much to figure out where I was going as to figure out where I had gotten to. (Maps from the map department at the Alabama Department of Transportation are one of the great bargains in state government. Among the offerings are road maps for every county, $2.25 to $3.75, depending on scale. You can buy them at the Department of Transportation, 1409 2270 West Gunter Park Drive, Montgomery, or you can order them via the Internet at http://www.dot.state.al.us/eqweb/general_maps.htm)

I carried my cell phone, too, and I thought it was a plus that I spent most of the morning in places where there wasn't a signal.

My wandering took me past old graveyards and country churches, large new homes and empty shacks falling in upon themselves, down roads so narrow they didn't have a stripe. Some of those petered out and became red clay.

One thing I didn't see was traffic. When you spend all of your time driving on busy roads, you forget that there are places where you can drive for miles without encountering another vehicle.

There were still things I could do, should do, when I got home.

But I did find the answer to my question. Taking a ride is still fun.

Learning to Quit

March 2004

I DO NOT REMEMBER when I learned how to read.

I remember a little more clearly when I learned how to stop reading.

Both experiences were liberating.

I can't recall the mechanics of learning to read; I certainly don't recall whether the teachers used phonics or look-say or whatever other method there might have been. I just know that reading seemed as natural as breathing.

Books became a magic carpet that I still ride. I recall walking a couple of miles into town with a dollar I had saved to buy a copy of Treasure Island. I can remember some of my favorite authors in elementary and junior high school. Not long ago I checked on the Internet to see whether I could find old books by one of them, Stephen W. Meader. I could, and I found that books I had checked out of the school library now are collectors' items with prices that reflect that fact. I did not buy one, but I did find that some of his fans are republishing some of his books.

Our family moved often when I was a child, and in every new

town the public library became a haven for me.

If reading brought pleasure, though, it also imposed a burden.

Nobody ever told me directly, but I somehow adopted the notion that once you started reading a book, you were honor bound to finish it. Perhaps the book police were out there keeping an eye on you.

I cannot tell you how many books over the years have been more like castor oil than elixir.

The unwritten rule applied to fiction. Bad story? Poor plotting? Slog on through it. Just don't pick up any more books by that author.

It applied to nonfiction. I pick up a work of nonfiction because I think it contains something that I want to know or ought to know. Most of those books have been worthwhile, but there were many that were not.

I sometimes found myself ensnared in verbiage so thick that I thought I would suffocate.

I do most of my reading in the evening. If the book were a particularly onerous one, I would manage only few pages before my eyes got heavy and the book slipped from my hands. Occasionally I would sneak in the reading of an enjoyable book concurrently with the heavier tome, but I always soldiered on, sometimes it seemed for months, until the book was finished.

I wish I could remember the title of the book that set me free. It was a dense social commentary of some sort. Whatever it was, I realized that I wasn't enjoying it, wasn't getting anything particularly rewarding from it, and I just put the book down.

I didn't pick it up again other than to return it to the shelf in the bookcase. That was the end of my deference to a self-imposed law, and I put down other books.

Some of them still sit on my bookshelf—perhaps at another time they might be more interesting—but I've given many others to an under funded public library to either sell or put in circulation.

I had never shared my compulsion—nor my little rebellion—with anyone until recently.

The people at my table at a civic club luncheon were talking about books they'd been reading. Someone mentioned a book that he had not liked; a woman at the table agreed. Both agreed, though, that they liked a recent book by the same author.

I sheepishly admitted that I had only lately learned that it was okay to start a book and not finish it. One of the women at the table said that was something she had just learned, too; one of the men said his wife still hadn't accepted that.

It was a comfort to learn that I hadn't been alone in my feelings.

I just hope the book police don't find out.

Okay, I'm a Packrat

April 2004

I CLEANED OUT a dresser drawer recently and came face to face with a discomfiting truth: I am a packrat.

I don't think of myself that way, but the evidence was indisputable.

As I sorted through the drawer, I wondered whether I should blame heredity or environment. Both, I suspect.

Recycling, although they didn't call it that, was a way of life on my grandparents' farm where I spent many of my formative years.

My grandmother saved anything that might have some conceivable use. She wound string that sealed a 25-pound bag of flour into a ball. She saved empty jars—the water jug my grandfather took to the field with him originally held a gallon of syrup. It was wrapped in a heavy paper bag that once held 10 pounds of sugar.

Of course my grandfather didn't throw anything away, either. Beneath a large old pine tree near the mule barn was a repository for broken plows and other equipment. From the pile, he cannibalized parts to keep other equipment running. When he needed a little folding money, he hauled some of the scrap iron to town to sell.

The pile was a treasure trove for young boys, too. Perhaps that's where I learned not to throw anything away if there was a place to put it.

We built all kinds of things with items from that scrap pile, including a mule wagon that nearly killed old Laura, but that's another story.

Certainly my grandparents were not unique in their thrift. All of the farms around us had outbuildings that were packed with old furniture, old clothing, and all manner of things that you didn't need at the moment but might need again some day.

So, the accumulation of stuff in that drawer wasn't my fault.

It was quite an inventory: Shoe laces that don't fit any of my shoes. Spare buttons for clothing that has long since worn out. A plastic package containing screws and a bracket that apparently were to mount something on the wall—I have no idea what. A watch whose battery has long since died. Several pairs of old glasses, none of which bring anything into focus anymore. Three marbles —two blue ones and one clear. A 1971 silver dollar.

And keys, lots and lots of keys; I have no idea what they might fit. The best way to find out, I thought, is to throw them away. So instead they went into the box of things I was saving.

When I finished, I realized that I had thrown hardly anything away.

If that one cardboard box represented all of my clutter, I could, perhaps excuse myself.

But I thought about the drawers in the old roll top desk in my study. Old pens that no longer write. Business cards from people whom I am unable to recall. Items I've torn from a newspaper or magazine; I must have thought they were important at the time.

And the utility room isn't any better. Old drill bits so dull they wouldn't bore a hole in dirt. Worn out files; they're good steel, might make a knife out of them some day. A pair of speakers that came out of a broken boom box. Instruction manuals for appliances that wore out long ago.

Actually, there are times when I've needed something that I knew I had, or was pretty sure I had, like a paint scraper, but it was easier to go to the store and buy a new one than to spend an hour or two looking for it.

And I don't even want to think about the attic, which is where I put the box of items from the dresser drawer.

Many years ago, my wife, our two sons and I lived for a while on a boat.

The space on a boat is finite. If you buy something new, you usually have to get rid of something old.

One of these days I've got to get rid of some of the clutter— starting with the box of stuff I took out of the dresser drawer; perhaps more importantly, I must learn to stop adding to the accumulation.

Or maybe we just ought to move onto a boat again.

Interchanges Look the Same

April 2004

IF SOMEONE PLUCKED you up and set you down in an automobile on an interstate highway, would you have any idea where you were?

I'd guess not. If it were dark, when you can't tell much about the topography, you could be anywhere in the country. Most of the signs clustered at the interchanges are, well, interchangeable: the same gasoline stations, the same fast food places, the same motels. In the daytime you could at least tell whether you are in mountains or plains or deserts.

Predictability has some merits, but too much of it leads to boredom.

It's not just the interstates that have become a succession of sameness.

At one time, major highways ran right through the middle of towns, and each town had its own landmarks, its own character.

Now we have bypasses around even small towns, and, as could have been expected, businesses migrated to the bypasses. Often they leave empty buildings in what had been a thriving town center. Except for a city limits sign or a welcome to wherever sign, these bypasses all look the same. There are the same businesses that you see at the interstate exits plus tire stores and car lots and strip malls.

You can drive past my little home town on U.S. 280 and not even be aware that there's an interesting town just a couple of blocks away.

Perhaps initially the sameness brought a certain amount of comfort.

When you pull into a Holiday Inn or a McDonald's, you have a pretty good idea of what it is going to be like.

It was different before the chaining of America's eating and sleeping establishments, before there was an interstate highway to carry you almost everywhere, travel was less certain and demanded a little more planning.

It was important to know where you were going to spend the night. With no nationally branded motels in every town, you couldn't count on there being suitable accommodations easily at hand.

That was why an American Automobile Association travel guide was almost as important as a road map. Armed with the AAA publication, you could make reservations at a motel whose name you'd never heard with some assurance that the accommodations would match the description in the book.

Eating was a little more of an adventure, too. You picked out a place that seemed to have a lot of cars in front or asked at the motel or a gas station. Sometimes a friend recommended a place along your route.

You could be pretty sure the food wasn't going to be just like that at the last place you ate, or at the next one. Sometimes the food was bad; sometimes it was surprisingly good.

When we were traveling with children, of course, predictability was a plus. Life was much more pleasant for everyone if we knew where we were going to stay and that the place would be acceptable.

With children, predictability in food is a blessing.

Now that most of our travels don't involve children, uniformity in food and lodging is just boring.

Sometimes schedules or business commitments demand that we stay at one of the same old places. When we can, though, we try to look for variety, perhaps a bed and breakfast place. B&B's are rarely located at an interstate exit or along a bypass, so we get an opportunity to see what a place is really like.

And it's fun to try a restaurant or café where the menu doesn't look exactly like the one at a spot just down the road.

I think the trips that we remember most are those to places that had their own identities.

There are still such places, if we look. Meanwhile, I wonder how many towns realize that they are dying a slow death by allowing themselves to look like every other town.

What I Want and What I Need

April 2004

OCCASIONALLY I FIND myself considering the gap between what I want and what I truly need. Perhaps it is a sign of maturing to find that the gap is narrowing.

When I do think of such things, I realize that there aren't really that many things that are essential and that many of the things that are essential have nothing to do with possessions.

Those thoughts about wants and needs come at odd moments. Often they stir memories of my grandparents and the realization of how dramatically our society changed from their generation to mine. It has changed even more for the generations younger than mine.

When I am in the gym working up a sweat, I sometimes picture the incredulity that my farmer grandfather would express at someone paying good money to use their muscles. My grandmother would find it just as odd that a person would buy a small bottle of water that did not taste any better than that from the well at the end of the porch.

We seem to think that we need many things that my

111

grandparents never thought about.

I don't know that my grandfather ever went to a movie theater, though he did watch some television programs after broadcasts finally reached our small town in the mid 1950s. My grandmother went to only one movie that I know of; she took a bunch of us grandkids to the matinee to see Walt Disney's "Song of the South."

If my grandparents ever went out to eat, I don't know about it, unless you count dinner on the ground at cemetery working at our small church or the occasional fish fries under the trees down by the pond.

My grandfather used to take loads of water melons to South Louisiana to sell in the summer time. Once he drove out to Texas to help move us back to Louisiana. But he and my grandmother never took a vacation trip.

In my earliest memory of my grandparents' home, there was an old crank telephone hanging in the hall that ran down the middle of the house. Three other families shared the same telephone line. We have at least seven phones in our house. They didn't have a typewriter; we have three computers (not counting some that are so outdated they have no real use).

The sum total of their clothing could fit in the small closets— they were added as an afterthought—and the chest of drawers.

They were what some would term simple people. My grandfather finished grade school; my grandmother went through junior high school.

My grandfather could raise crops and cattle, build a barn and grind cane. My grandmother could raise chickens, kill, clean and cook one. She canned vegetables, smoked meat and sewed quilts.

Simple? Only in their wants.

I never heard either of them talk about anything they wanted that they didn't have, never got a hint that they'd been deprived.

When I am musing, I wonder whether their wants would be

greater if they were around today. Our whole economy seems to be built on increasing our wants. I've read that consumer spending accounts for more than two-thirds of our national economy.

The triumph of wants over needs was summed up in a bumper sticker that had some popularity a few years ago: "He who dies with the most toys wins."

Perhaps, but as I sort through things, it strikes me that very often the excess of our wants over our needs is a pretty accurate indicator of unhappiness.

Check Me Out of Self-Checkout

July 2004

I FINALLY BRAVED the self-checkout lane at one of those big box stores.

I was shopping with my daughter-in-law, who was visiting with us. She had a number of items in her basket. I had only a few.

We opted for the self-checkout because there weren't many lanes open that had living, breathing cashiers.

I had previously avoided the lanes on the theory that if they can train us to check ourselves out, pretty soon they'll have us unloading the trucks and stocking the shelves.

I found that I'd been right to avoid the self-checkout line. The process was not very satisfactory. It certainly was not as fast as dealing with a competent cashier.

The theory is simple. Every item in your cart has a bar code. You take the item from the cart, pass it over the scanner, which reads the item and the price, and put the item in a bag. Of course, if the scanner cannot read the bar code, you have to key it in yourself. You probably are much slower at that than an experienced cashier. If, heaven forbid, the bar code is missing, then a real person has to intervene.

When you wave your last item over the bar code scanner, you feed your money into a slot or swipe your credit card through a reader. In the case of cash, the machine emits your change. If you are using a credit card, you write your name on a pressure sensitive screen.

That's the theory. In our case, a live employee had to intervene several times during the process: Once to verify that my daughter-in-law was old enough to buy beer; another time because the scanner was stuck. Another time because the scanner recorded a price that was higher than the price listed on a sign where the item was displayed. And again to verify that my daughter-in-law was indeed the holder of the credit card that she passed through the card reader.

(I suppose the rationale behind self-checkout is that if the customers do more of the work, the store can have even fewer minimum wage employees working part-time so that the company doesn't have to pay benefits. Lower payroll costs, we are told, helps bring lower prices so that people who aren't paid very much money can afford to buy things. There seems to be some paradox in all of this, but I'm sure the economists—none of whom, I would bet, work for minimum wage—can explain it.)

If price is the only consideration, then I guess all of this is a good thing.

But as I was standing there taking it all in, I considered my hometown hardware store.

It's owned and operated by Steve Moore, who lives right there in town.

It's an old fashioned sort of place. The wooden counters in the center of the store are old and well worn. On the counter is a cash register and an adding machine—the kind that cranks out a paper tape. There's not a bar code reader in sight. Steve doesn't need one; he knows how much nearly everything costs. There is a credit card scanner, but even it doesn't have a dedicated phone line.

You can buy three screws, a few feet of rope or a handful of nails without them coming in a package that takes you 10 minutes to open.

If you tell Steve what it is that you're trying to do—or trying to fix—he'll take time help you. I've known him to spend 20 or 30 minutes helping someone figure out how to repair something and to sell only a few dollars worth of merchandise in the process.

I plead to being old fashioned, but I like having a place like that around. So I buy there as often as I can. Sometimes I know that I could get the same item at one of the mega stores 30 minutes or so down the road for a few dollars less.

Watching where our money goes is important, but value isn't always measured by price alone.

Happiness Is a Hammock

August 2004

IT IS HARD not to be contented in a hammock.

When a few cool days passed through recently—my Minnesota friend would laugh at our definition of cool—it seemed a waste not to be outdoors, so on a Saturday afternoon my wife and I strung the hammocks under the trees near the water's edge.

We equipped ourselves with a book and a pillow; it is obligatory, I think, to pretend that you are going to lie in the hammock and read.

Not many pages got turned in either hammock.

There is something about being cradled, suspended in air, that invites you to let the open book drop to your chest and rest your eyes for a moment. Perhaps the insides of our heads are like those in the dolls my sister had when we were kids. The eyes were connected to a rod and a weight inside the head. Whenever the doll was put down on its back, the rod moved and the doll's eyes closed.

In a hammock, when your eyes close, the breeze tickles your cheek and arms and legs, and sounds seem to recede.

You drift into sleep and float back to consciousness without opening your eyes, aware that you have been asleep and that you are going back to sleep.

And you are just awake enough to be aware that what you are doing is wonderful.

For some reason, time doesn't seem to matter in a hammock. You think about getting up, but it is difficult to think of a good reason not to linger.

The cool spell has passed, and the heat and humidity have returned. I removed the hammocks from under the trees to keep them from mildewing.

But fall will come—the sourwood leaves are already turning, and I picked up a gum leaf the other day that was the color of a golden delicious apple. What better thing is there to do on an autumn afternoon than kick back in the hammock listening to a football game on the radio?

Our hammocks are of the cotton rope variety that generally is identified with Pawley's Island in South Carolina. We like them because they allow plenty of air circulation, but there are hammocks of every description. As with so many things that seem to be attuned with nature, hammocks are said to have originated with the natives of the Western Hemisphere. They are said to have been an invention of the Mayas, with the first ones being made from the bark of the Hamak tree. From there they spread along trade routes north and south.

European explorers who were looking for gold recognized another kind of treasure when they saw it and took hammocks home with them.

Most of us got a greater benefit from the hammocks they took than from the gold they plundered, although we could claim that hammocks have a corrupting influence.

I am one of those people who feels guilty if he is not doing something productive; it is a trait that I am trying to overcome.

I ran across an interesting quote from Cicero the other day that helps: "He does not seem to me to be a free man who does not sometimes do nothing."

Who am I to argue with Cicero? On to the hammock.

Thanks Because We Need To

November 2004

IT'S THE TIME of year when we pause to reflect, however briefly, on the things we're thankful for. Then we begin making the list of things we wish for.

My list of things I'm thankful for is a lot longer than my list of things I wish for. It has been that way for a while now, and when I mentally count the things that I am thankful for, relationships far outnumber possessions.

I would like to think that this is an indication of some maturity. I suspect that it may be an indication of recognition of my own mortality. That recognition, I suppose, is one element of maturity.

It would be different, I'm sure, if I had to worry each day about food or shelter or clothing. Those things would top my wish list and, if I got them, my gratitude list.

And the things that we think are important and are thankful for changes as we go along. Even so, I am confident that the bumper sticker that was popular a few years ago—He who dies with the most toys wins—is wrong.

Toys are nice. If I tried, I could make a long list of them that would be nice to have. But I don't feel less content because I don't have them, and I have learned that the new wears off of possessions.

The new doesn't wear off the things that I am truly thankful for: a morning sunrise, mist over the lake, a bird's song, and, especially, the feeling of belonging to a family and a community.

It is appropriate that the Thanksgiving celebration centers on the family, because for many people, including me, family tops the list.

Thanksgiving is a different kind of holiday in many ways. It doesn't fall on the same date each year; unlike many holidays, it does not celebrate a person or event.

In fact, historians say that our picture of Thanksgiving is somewhat romanticized. Our popular notion of the First Thanksgiving being celebrated by the Pilgrims in 1621 is a myth, they say. That event was really just a harvest festival, and it wasn't repeated the next year.

Though it is now disputed, I have read that the first official American Thanksgiving is said to have been in 1676 in Charlestown, Mass. A proclamation adopted by the town's governing body on June 20 recited that God had "brought to pass bitter things against his own Covenant people in this wilderness" but that he had "remembered mercy."

In the words of the proclamation, "The Council has thought meet to appoint and set apart the 29th day of this instant June, as a day of Solemn Thanksgiving and praise to God for such his Goodness and Favour, many Particulars of which mercy might be Instanced, but we doubt not those who are sensible of God's Afflictions, have been as diligent to espy him returning to us … ."

Whether we believe in Divine Providence or just in blind fortune, most of us have much more to be thankful for than did those folks in Plymouth and Charlestown.

In this fast paced world, we seem to spend more time looking to the future than in looking back; that is human nature. It also seems to be human nature to stop occasionally to balance the bitter things we have endured against the mercy we have received.

We observe Thanksgiving because we need to.

Reality and Miracles

November 2004

THE CHRISTMAS CATALOGS have begun arriving in the mail, prompting our annual complaints to ourselves and to each other about the shopping season starting earlier each year. Catalogs come so often throughout the year, though, that the only thing that really distinguishes the current batch is the holiday themes on the covers.

I still look through them, more often to find things to give as gifts than to find something to wish for.

There was a time, though, when the Christmas catalogs really were wish books. My sister and I (and a little later, my younger brother) would wait eagerly for the arrival of the catalogs from Sears and from Montgomery Ward. There were enticements on every page of toys, and we turned those pages until we nearly wore them out. Sometimes we would argue about whose turn it was to look at a catalog.

Children then were not subjected to the steady barrage of marketing that occurs today. There was no television, and thus no daily kiddy shows telling us what every kid ought to have.

There were some sales pitches to kids on the afternoon radio shows that we listened to, but they were for relatively benign things like Ovaltine and cereal. I do remember falling prey to some of that marketing, talking my mom into buying shredded wheat because inside each box were neat cards filled with Indian lore. I didn't really like shredded wheat, and after a couple of boxes of the stuff sat on the shelf long enough to lose their crunch, my mother resisted my pleas for her to buy more.

It was those Christmas catalogs, though, that stirred our imaginations—and our greed. What fun we could have with this toy or that. We made and remade our lists. Who could resist such an array of possibilities?

But most of those childhood Christmases were during tough times, and there was a wide gap between wishing and getting. Occasionally we would get one thing that was on our wish lists. As often, though, what was under the tree on Christmas morning bore no resemblance to what had been in our dreams the night before.

It was just before Christmas in a particularly difficult year that my older sister disabused me of the notion that presents appeared under the tree by magic. I shouldn't count on getting any of the large presents on my wish list, she said.

She told me this because she didn't want to see me crushed on Christmas morning.

She was right, of course.

But it is hard to tell a kid not to want, no matter how tough the times are.

Some children will go to bed this Christmas Eve fervently believing in miracles. Others will go to bed expecting nothing, their acquaintance with reality belying their years.

My sister was wrong, too. That there were presents under the tree at all was a minor miracle. They appeared because there were people who knew about children and wishes and who cared.

There still are.

There's not a community where there isn't at least one person or group seeking to ensure that kids with slim hopes will experience a small miracle on Christmas morn.

Church groups make the miracle. So do cops and firemen and welfare workers, civic clubs and the Marine Corps League.

They've learned that having a hand in making a miracle can be as gratifying as receiving one.

It's Not Our Accents

December 2004

ALTHOUGH I HAVE lived in the South all of my life, I think of myself as being reasonably sophisticated. I grew up in small towns and live in a small town now, but in between, I lived in several cities. And I did spend a fair number of years in parts of Florida that are southern only in geography.

I generally speak grammatical English, and my accent doesn't automatically brand me a Dixie native.

But it is not our accents that give us away. It is our words.

Even in the age of mass media, when a good portion of our regional vocabulary is yielding to a national syntax, some regional peculiarities remain.

I started thinking about our native vocabulary some months ago when I got a note from Jerry Brown, a south Alabama native who is dean of the school of journalism at the University of Montana. Jerry —who no one in Montana would mistake for being a local—sent along a piece about disappearing words and phrases. He started a list with a couple of phrases—sweet milk and light bread—and invited me to come up with others.

126

Jerry's two phrases stirred memories. In the country, including at my grandparents' house, many folks kept a milk cow, and nearly everyone kept regular milk, identified as sweet milk, and butter milk in the refrigerator. You had to specify which kind of milk you wanted. Light bread was store bought or sto' boughten (another disappearing phrase) as opposed to corn bread. The occasional supper of sandwiches made with light bread was a real treat. (Supper was, of course, the evening meal. Most often it consisted of leftovers from dinner, which was the big meal served in the middle of the day.) After dinner, my grandmother would leave the bowls of vegetables and the corn bread on the table, spreading a table cloth over them to keep the flies away. Supper was eaten cold.

Cornbread crumbled into a glass of butter milk was a treat for some people, the equivalent of today's smoothies, but I never developed a taste for it.

We hardly ever say sweet milk or light bread anymore.

Now we ask for sweet tea or unsweet. We even specify whether we want iced tea or hot tea. In the South of my youth those weren't ready options; all tea was iced and all tea was sweet.

If bread and milk were described in specifics, quantities were often less certain.

Folks would cook a "mess" of turnip greens. When you'd eaten all you could, you'd had a bate of greens. (Bate – I don't know that I've ever seen the word written down, so I don't know about my spelling—was sometimes used to describe being fed up, as in "I've had a bate of your meddling.")

There was another way to describe a sufficiency: All you could say grace over. I still recall my grandmother saying, "I'll put these trays in the refrigerator and pretty soon we'll have all the ice we can say grace over."

Other words come to mind. The small pieces of fat pine that you used to kindle a fire were splinters, and the stuff you fueled a lamp or a lantern with was coal oil.

Our language painted pictures of ordinary life. If someone was mad as a wet hen, you didn't want to be around them, and if you'd ever seen a mule eating briars, you knew what grinning like a mule eating briars meant.

Some words didn't mean what they seemed. If someone said they would be there "directly," that didn't mean to look for them right away. They'd be there after while.

Even in the South, of course, we had our regional differences.

I was practically grown before I knew what French toast was. In my home, it was lost bread, a translation of the south Louisiana French pain perdu. Burlap bags were poke sacks, croaker sacks, or tow sacks, depending on where you were from. And what was called a hose in one place was called a hose pipe in others.

One remembered word or phrase brings another.

No matter how homogenized our national vocabulary becomes, though, there is one word that will eventually give a Southerner away.

No matter how long he has been gone from the South or how many degrees she has, sooner or later, he or she will tell someone, "I'm fixing to ...."

We Really Are Colorful

December 2004

WE SOUTHERNERS DON'T think of our vocabularies as being quaint or colorful; we find that the words we employ are useful ways of communicating information, ideas and feelings.

If we try to put ourselves in an outsider's shoes, though, we have to admit that some of our words and expressions are, well, colorful.

When I wrote recently about our vocabulary, some of which borders on extinction, I knew I was hitting only a few highlights. And I knew that people would be reminded of other ways in which we express ourselves.

I heard from many of you.

I wrote about the word "mess" as a description of quantity, as in a mess of greens. David Burrier of Dothan reminded me of another meaning. He's originally from Oklahoma and his wife is from Chicago. "It almost caused a neighbor to get whacked by my wife when she said our two-year-old 'is such a mess.'" People who grew up in the South would know the neighbor was paying a compliment.

Judith Howard from Ruston, La., reported that a visitor from

California was most intrigued by "might could." Wrote Judith, "I noticed when I lived out of the South, when I slipped and said 'I might could...' it always drew a comment.

She remembered her father calling a blouse a "waist," a term I remember from childhood, and her father referring to a "skeeter bar," another one I remember. For the uninitiated, a skeeter bar is the canopy of netting you put around a bed to keep the mosquitoes at bay.

She chided me for putting the g on the end of fixin'. I hope she didn't think I was putting on airs.

Jane Garing, who was born in Oklahoma, but who has lived in Alabama since she was 5, recalled her grandfather from Clay County always said someone lived "down the road a piece." If he felt well, he said he "felt tolable."

Jane said she uses the word "yonder" often, much to the amusement of her grandchildren. My brother, who lives in our hometown in Louisiana, recalls that when he was in the Navy and used the expression "over yonder," his fellow sailors would hoot. "Brown, where the heck is over yonder."

But, as Jane points out, the Air Force song refers to the "wild blue yonder" and there's a Baptist (Southern, of course) hymn, "When the Roll Is Called Up Yonder."

From Palmer, Alaska, Emilie Beasley wrote that although she has lived in the northernmost state since 1977, she hasn't lost her Southern drawl. She's raising two grandsons, and when they forget to do their chores, she threatens to "put the guineas in behind them."

My cousin's grandfather kept guinea fowl—we called them guinea hens—and they were better at guarding the house than a watchdog.

Emilie and her husband have land in Talladega County where they plan to settle one day. We won't have any trouble understanding her. She might even have guineas.

Don and Nancy Carlisle of Dadeville reminded me that when someone asks you to "crack the window" they don't mean use a hammer.

They also reminded me that when you "run into" somebody, it doesn't necessarily mean you had a wreck. And they couldn't remember how many times they'd heard that somebody "up and died."

I'm sure many of us have used the expression "stepping in high cotton" without ever having seen anyone doing it. But we know what it means.

And I'm told of a Tallapoosa County physician—not from around here, of course—who excused himself to ask his receptionist what a patient meant when he said he had a "risin'." (I hope I'm spelling that right. I always heard it, but I never saw it written down.)

One of these days our vocabulary might become as homogenized as so much of our commerce has become. If it does, our language will have lost some of its vigor.

I wrote in the last column that no matter whether you lose your Southern accent and spend decades away from your home ground, sooner or later you'll give your origins away by saying "I'm fixing to ...."

There's another giveaway.

Have you ever gotten on an elevator in some distant locale and asked someone to mash the button for your floor?

Some Day Doesn't Arrive

January 2004

I DON'T PUT a lot of stock in New Year's resolutions, feeling that they represent, as Samuel Johnson said of second marriages, the triumph of hope over experience. Vague vows that we will get more exercise or save more money are likely the same promises we made a year earlier.

Barring the rare miracle, we begin the new year as the same person who ended the old one. We have the same strengths and weaknesses, hopes and fears. About the only change that turning the leaf on the calendar makes is that we are a day older.

Despite my reluctance to indulge in the New Year's list making, I know from experience that there is something to be said for putting a goal in writing. The very act of putting it down in black and white seems to lend some reality to a goal.

Perhaps the end of the holiday season—when we're thinking about the money we shouldn't have spent and the food we shouldn't have eaten—is not the best time to be making goals anyway. New Year's resolutions often seem more the product of remorse than desire.

Simply writing a goal down—no matter how specifically it's defined—won't make it happen. It remains a wish unless there is a date, a deadline , built into it. "I will save $500 by July 1" is a lot more specific and measurable than "I will save more."

There's another catch in translating the goal into reality. The goal and the deadline have to be where they can be seen regularly. If it's stuck out of sight in a desk drawer, it disappears.

Of course, none of this works unless the goal is something that is really important to begin with.

A young woman with whom I worked years ago knew that we had taken an extended time off to live on a boat in England and Holland. She talked about wanting to go to Greece, not just on a two-week vacation, but for months.

Her desire, though, was always expressed as "one of these days I want to go to Greece."

One of these days, though, never got any closer until she wrote down the date on which she would get on the plane.

After she did that—or because she did it—things fell into place. She made a check list of the things that she needed to do before her departure.

She figured out how much money she would need to get by and what she could do without in order to save it. She figured out what she would need in the way of clothing and lined up a place to stay. She got her passport and reserved her airline tickets.

All of this was long before the Internet, and the preparation became part of the adventure.

Every time she checked an item off the list, the dream became more real.

Perhaps the fact that she was in the newspaper business and was accustomed to meeting deadlines helped, because on her selected date, she actually departed.

She had a date in mind for coming home, too, but it was less fixed. She was having such a good time that she found part-time jobs to support herself, and her six-month sojourn became a year.

As she had planned, she returned to the United States and went back into the newspaper business.

She died a couple of years ago at much too young an age.

But she had turned a "some day" dream into reality while she had an opportunity.

Back in the Game

March 2004

CHALK ONE up for the squirrel.

He's not winning, but at least he's back in the game.

We have been adversaries—the squirrel and I—for many months. I put up a bird feeder. He finds a way to loot it. Sometimes he's found a way to break into the feeder; other times he's made off with the entire feeder.

Then last year, a friend told me about a feeder he'd bought that seemed to work. It's essentially a square plastic tube with small holes through which the birds can nibble on seeds. Outside the plastic tube there is a square metal shield with perching places. It's suspended by a spring. When anything heavier than a bird lands on one of the perches, the metal shield drops down, covering the feeding holes.

I bought one with little confidence that it would keep the squirrel at bay. I figured that if the squirrel could get to it, he would simply make off with it and chew away at the plastic until he got to the food.

The trick, I thought, was keeping the squirrel from getting to it.

135

So I attached a small pulley to the end of a piece of clothes line wire, threaded a thin cord through the pulley, and managed to pass the wire over the limb of a tree that stands just outside our dining room window. I fastened the other end of the wire to a hook.

I tied the new feeder to the cord, filled it with seed and hoisted it aloft. The feeder hangs about three feet below the limb and about 15 feet above the ground.

For months I watched a very frustrated squirrel. He raced up and down the tree trunk, out the limb and back again, calculating angles and trajectories. He sat on the twig-sized limb of a smaller tree nearby, trying to decide whether he could catapult himself onto the feeder.

He spent a lot of time poised on the limb right above the feeder, twitching the way squirrels do when they're contemplating snatching a bite of food. He clamped his rear feet onto the tree limb and tried to stretch down along the cord to reach the feeder. It was just out of reach.

The birds munched happily on their seed while the squirrel found other things to eat.

He'd given up, I thought.

I should have known better.

I was upstairs when my wife summoned me over the intercom.

"Come look out the dining room window," she said.

At last he had done it.

There, eight feet outside the dining room window, he was wrapped around the feeder like a teen-age boy around his girl friend. I wish I could have seen how he got there.

He wasn't getting anything to eat; the shutter had done its job. He was simply hanging on and trying to figure out what to do next.

His attention was so fixed that he didn't see me at the window until I tapped on the glass.

He was so startled that he turned loose. At the last moment he seemed to consider trying to jump to the tree trunk, but it was too late and he plunged the 15 feet to the ground.

He was unfazed. He didn't even stop to catch his breath before he disappeared behind the tree.

I haven't seen the squirrel out on the limb above the feeder sine then, but I am not fooled. He's out there somewhere studying engineering drawings and plotting his strategy.

And I'm like a Chicago Cubs fan watching my team cling to a narrow lead in the late innings: I know that sooner or later something bad is going to happen.

A Good Thing We Had

May 2005

ONE THING HASN'T changed over the years: the first day of summer. Summer doesn't begin on some arbitrary date on the calendar. It begins the day that school is out.

The nature of summer has changed for school kids, but not the near universal approval of its arrival.

Looking back, that delicious interval when you were big enough to be out of your parents' sight and not yet old enough to get a summer job, may have offered as much freedom as anyone is likely to have.

Of course more moms were home then, so that meant kids could be home, too. Today we have fashioned an economy in which both spouses (if there are two in the household) work, either because they wish to or feel that they must in order to support a certain lifestyle.

If there are children in the household, that means day care or other organized activity. (Some young people get left home alone during the day, but that's a whole other and scary story.)

Even in families where one of the adults is at home during the

138

day, life for the children is more organized than it once was. That's not intended as criticism. Life has changed, and will change again. In their organized activities perhaps the kids gain knowledge and learn skills an earlier generation of kids didn't have.

I do wonder, though, whether those kids would know what to do if someone wasn't organizing their time for them. (Okay, they'd watch television or play video games. We'd probably have done that, too, except that television and video games weren't around.)

Since most homes weren't air conditioned, much of what we found to do was outdoors.

It was not such a fearful age, and we could roam on our bicycles without a destination or a deadline. Bicycles provided that first real taste of freedom. Our parents (or our neighbors and kin) often didn't know exactly where we were, and they didn't worry as long as we turned up by supper time.

The games we organized didn't have adults coaching us, enforcing rules, or judging us. We learned a good deal about give and take, even if we didn't hone the skills the average little leaguer of today possesses.

Still, anyone who tells you that there weren't boring times, especially as the summer wore on, has a selective memory.

If we were bored, though, it was our problem to deal with. Our parents didn't automatically plunk us into some organized activity.

Dealing with boredom was educational in itself. We had to invent our own things to do, whether it was solo or with our buddies.

Sometimes, lying on your back in the shade of a big old oak tree wasn't a bad way to deal with boredom. As you let your mind wander, you tended to forget you were bored anyway.

Most of the time, though, there were friends and cousins around, and someone always could cook up something.

We dug worms in the chicken yard and went fishing. We weren't really patient enough to be fishermen, but it was a way of emulating the grownups.

We liberated boards and nails and tools from our parents and grandparents and built forts in the woods. We learned how to hammer and saw. We also learned about poison ivy. My cousin's grandfather said we must have thought tools grew out of the ground because we'd planted his all over creation

We stuffed ourselves on blackberries right from the vine. We learned about chiggers.

We put a floor in the cupola of the hay barn. It was a wonderful perch from which to view the world until my grandfather found out about the project. We learned about the dangers of spontaneous combustion.

We cobbled together a wagon and hitched the mule to it. When the mule tired of the wagon tongue hitting her heels, she bolted, scattering pieces of the wagon over the back field before she cleared the fence. We learned the next day that the grownups knew more about what we were doing than we thought.

We ended our summers knowing about many things.

But what we did not know was what a good—and fleeting— thing we had.

Pop Quiz on Patience

May 2004

I HAVE BEEN trying to learn patience. Although my children probably would have suggested that I start in a remedial class, I like to think of my effort as continuing education.

I didn't know that there would be a pop test last week.

We were welcoming a new member of our community, and a general invitation was extended for a get acquainted lunch.

We gathered at an area eating spot. There wasn't a big crowd yet.

We placed our orders. We visited as we waited for our food. And we visited. And we waited.

Finally orders began arriving, but they came in ones and twos, with long intervals between those arrivals. Several people who had ordered one of the specials were told after they sat there waiting that the kitchen had run out of the special. These folks had ordered at noon. Perhaps the restaurant wasn't really expecting anyone to drop in for lunch.

There did not seem to be any correlation between when someone had ordered and when the food actually arrived. Those who were served first waited for a while before eating. When it became obvious that this was to be a drawn out affair, they went ahead with their meals.

In an earlier time, I would have long since departed, probably after making certain the management knew of its shortcomings. When our children saw me looking at my watch in a restaurant, they braced themselves for the scene they knew was coming.

But I have been practicing, and on this day, I sat and waited and chatted with my tablemates. The fellowship was good, even if the service wasn't.

After a while, though, conversation wound down.

Most of our group had been served and had finished eating.

About 45 minutes after placing our orders, three of us were still waiting. I headed to the counter to ask for my money back—it's one of those places where you pay when you order. A peanut butter sandwich at home would be just fine, I thought.

As I approached the counter, though, my sandwich came up.

I earned my passing grade when I simply took the plate and returned to the table. The food for the two remaining hungry souls arrived shortly afterwards.

The three of us ate while the others visited and prepared to depart.

After the last of the food arrived, we all got a half-hearted kind of apology for the delays. The attitude was "we're a small outfit, so what can you expect?"

I kept my mouth shut. Clinched shut. One of the things I thought was that it's likely to remain a small outfit, if it remains at all.

All things considered, I would give myself a solid B on the pop quiz. The other two people who sat and watched the others get served and eat earned B pluses or better.

Although I passed, I think I may have gotten more satisfaction out of getting an F.

A Feline Welfare State

July 2004

YELLOW CAT AND I have seen altruism morph into its own version of a welfare state.

We have seen that change the relationship between the giver and the recipient, and neither of us has been very comfortable with it.

Yellow Cat is not my cat, but I have been feeding him for some time now, and when he has gotten sick, I have paid for his medical care. He does not regard that as giving me a claim on his life.

Yellow Cat—we didn't hang that name/description on him until later—lurked around our area for a long time before we established a relationship. Our understanding is straightforward: I take care of him; he does what he darn well pleases.

That relationship has had its strains, most notably when my side of the bargain has included a trip to the vet.

In recent weeks I noticed that Yellow Cat was not eating much from his dish and was in general making himself scarce, but I attributed that to our having so many visitors around.

On July 4, I saw Yellow Cat's tail protruding from the small opening at the end of the steps from the side deck to the door. It's a place where he often takes refuge. I tweaked his tail, but there was no response. I did it again, and the tail twitched very, very slowly and lay still again.

I grabbed a hammer and a crow bar to pry up the step. As I pried, I could see Yellow Cat lying on his side, barely moving. Ordinarily the hammering would have propelled him from under the step like a shot.

He didn't resist when I picked him up and put him in the cat carrier. I put some water before him and he lapped it up for a long time.

That Monday, I took Yellow Cat to the veterinarian's office. He stayed there two nights awaiting the blood test that showed an infection but no other serious ailments. When I collected Yellow Cat, the vet gave me a bottle of antibiotics to administer twice a day.

We still had guests, so I couldn't confine Yellow Cat in the house.

The first couple of days when he came to his food dish he allowed me to pick him up and squirt medicine down his throat. As he began to feel better, though, he was less agreeable. He'd peer through the glass door at feeding time, but he would retreat when I brought the dish out.

That's when the welfare state mentality took over.

"No medicine, no food," I said and took the dish inside.

He continued to show up every day at meal time, but he wouldn't let me catch him. I would sit on the step by the dish and he would sit at the end of the deck watching.

I would wait; he would wait. Then I would take the dish inside.

I have invested considerable money in a cat's health care, and I know what is good for him better than he does, just as I often know what is good for other people better than they do themselves. But cats and people don't always want to do what we think is best.

I realized that what had started as an altruistic impulse was becoming an effort to control and that Yellow Cat was not willing to trade food for freedom.

So if I can, I will give Yellow Cat his medicine. If I can't, though, I won't stop putting his food dish out. Sometimes you have to do what little good you can instead of what you think the larger good would be.

Heaven on Light Bread

July 2004

HERE IT IS the end of July and I had not realized until the other night that I had not had a truly tasty tomato this summer.

The best tomatoes are homegrown, but there's no room for a real garden on our half hill: too much slope, too much shade.

I appropriated some flower bed space for a few plants. There are a couple of basil bushes, an eggplant, a parsley plant and a rosemary bush—the herb we use least—that is threatening to take over the entire bed. There is a pot with chives in it.

And there is a lone tomato plant. As usual, spring took me by surprise, and I didn't do much preparation before sticking the plant in the ground. It has repaid my lack of diligence by producing some small fruit that is better than store bought, but not outstanding.

Luckily, a neighbor's bounty reminded us of what real tomatoes taste like.

I almost missed the gift.

It was nearly dark when I got home on a recent evening. A plastic grocery bag leaned by the back door, tied closed.

We often use those bags as waste basket liners, and I assumed that my wife had put the bag there for me to take to the garbage can.

It was only by chance that I asked first.

The bag wasn't garbage. My wife had seen it when she arrived home, but her hands were full, so she had left it. She'd forgotten it was there.

I brought the bag in, and she untied it. Inside were tomatoes of medium size, obviously vine ripened. (I've found that giant tomatoes rarely have taste that matches their size.)

We changed our supper plans.

We had sliced tomatoes—they were so full of flavor that they didn't need mayonnaise, and the first bite transported me back to my grandmother's kitchen—a cantaloupe that was rich with flavor, and cold ham.

We did not know who had left the treasure. We were looking contentedly at our empty plates when our neighbor Ann called to make certain we'd found them. I was already planning the next day's lunch—the best summer lunch you can imagine: A tomato and onion and cheese sandwich.

There is a certain way to make such sandwiches:

You use white bread, untoasted. Just trust me on this.

Slather the bread—both pieces—with mayonnaise (some people use Miracle Whip, but that's a case study in itself).

Top one piece of the bread with a slice of American cheese and a couple of juicy tomato slices sprinkled with salt and pepper. Putting the cheese down first keeps the tomato from making the bread too soggy.

Add a slice of Vidalia onion and top it with the other slice of bread.

Eat it immediately. The bread gets soggy if you let it sit for long.

Wash it down with iced tea—sweet tea, of course,

Then get up and make another one.

There's a meat packer that advertises its bratwurst as heaven on a bun.

Around here, in the summertime, a good tomato and onion and cheese sandwich is heaven on light bread.

Guests and Broken Things

September 2004

THIS WAS THE summer when things broke.

It's a given that they break only when you want to use them. However, I've discovered another rule that seems to apply at our house: Things that people would really like to use break when we have house guests.

The application of that rule reached an all time high this summer, perhaps because we had more house guests for a longer period of time.

It started right after our older son and his family arrived for an extended stay. He had a good deal of accumulated leave he needed to use, and we were pleased that they wanted to spend the time at the lake.

A number of their friends were invited to come and stay for varying lengths of time while they were here.

Summer on the lake means outdoor activity, especially boating. That creates a big demand for ice. When we built the house, we installed a separate ice maker instead of relying on the refrigerator, and it always met the demand—until this summer. Shortly after the guests arrived, the ice bin was almost depleted. And the machine wasn't making any more ice.

Only a few weeks earlier, I had thrown away a bunch of plastic ice trays that we hadn't used for years.

The appliance repairman couldn't come for several days, so I bought new ice trays and bags of ice. The news when the repairman did come was not good. It would cost half the price of a new machine to fix the old one. We opted to replace it, but a new one wouldn't arrive for several weeks. We made do.

The blender was next. My daughter-in-law was making some kind of frozen drinks when it emitted a large spark and died. On the next trip to town, I bought a new one.

Then it was the runabout, which is in almost constant use when the children and grandchildren are here. The people at the boat shop must have sensed my desperation—when you have a house full of adults and children, you really want them to be entertained, preferably outdoors. Although the July 4 holiday was at hand, they managed to install a new starter and get the boat back to life—for a while.

The following week the alternator quit working. While the boat was in the shop for that, the ignition switch on our old pontoon boat went bad. I could not find an exact replacement, and the switch I bought had more wires than the old one did.

I had to guess which of the extra wires went where. Before closing everything back up, I turned the key. The engine turned over, and I congratulated myself on my handiwork. That was before I discovered that although the boat would start, it wouldn't stop. Obviously my guess about the wiring had been wrong, and the only way to kill the engine was to kink the fuel line until the engine died.

A house call from the boat mechanic took care of that.

Then Yellow Cat, the semi-domesticated cat who lives around

our house, got sick. A few days at the vet and some expensive medicine restored him to his usual form.

Finally, my truck began overheating.

Time and money took care of everything.

Nothing that had happened was anybody's fault, and I managed to handle it all with a certain degree of equanimity.

Taking a cue from my son the optimist, I decided that we were lucky that the air conditioning and the septic tank functioned without a problem.

The last of the guests departed, and life returned to normal.

Until last week

With company on the way, the upstairs air conditioning unit—the one that cools our bedroom—gave up the ghost. A new compressor had to be ordered.

I could even deal with that. Since there was only one guest, we could move into a downstairs bedroom where the air conditioning still worked.

Just to be on the safe side, though, I think I'll have the septic tank checked.

The Residue of What We Do

January 2005

THE WORD LEGACY has gotten a lot of use lately, sparked by the inauguration of George W. Bush to a second term as president.

It has been used in the sense of a thing handed down by a predecessor. Commentators have described his second-term initiatives as his attempt to shape his legacy. From what the historians say, two-term presidents use their second term to try to influence how they are judged by subsequent generations.

A legacy, though, isn't so easily built. The legacy of Lyndon Johnson's first full term prevented him from even seeking a second. He would have wanted, I am sure, for his presidency to be remembered for his efforts to bring full citizenship to all Americans and to fight poverty. That was overshadowed, though, by the legacy of the Vietnam War and the deep fissures it tore in American society.

Presidents and others in positions of power may concern themselves about what the history books will say.

Most of us will never figure in a history book—excepting, perhaps, a family genealogy—but we all leave a legacy, whether we intend to or not. If we were called on to say what that legacy will be, I suspect that most of us would get it wrong.

Last year our pastor, Dr. Robert Leverett, died unexpectedly and at far too young an age. Before he came to our congregation, he had been a district superintendent and had had a hand in building some churches much larger than ours. Perhaps that was his legacy for some.

But for us, his legacy is in the faces of those who line up at the Loaves and Fishes food pantry that he helped establish and in the joyful sound of children as they gather for the children's sermon each Sunday morning.

On occasions when our grown children are reminiscing (it's not just older folks who reminisce; they just have more to remember) we are surprised by the things in our lives that had an impact on them. They often are things that we would not have thought of as important, but they are part of our legacy.

Cindy Aman of Dothan spent years putting together a cookbook that she called "In Search of My Mother's Kitchen."

In it she says, "Who of us hasn't made a dish and referred to it as mother's cornbread, or Aunt Clarkie's coconut cake. Are these people from the past sitting on our shoulders? In a way, yes, they are. When we cook their recipes or refer to them and their recipes we are passing on more than food. We are passing on a culture, a heritage, a long line of memories, all tied up with food. What a powerful thing!"

That is a legacy.

And it reminded me of the legacy of my own grandparents. They probably never used the word legacy in their lives, but from my grandmother I learned a lot about patience, from my grandfather about doing what you are supposed to do, regardless of whether there's something else you'd rather be doing. Their legacies, like most legacies, were not in the words they said but in the lives they lived, unremarked by the history books, but creating the most important kind of history.

In her cookbook, Aman quotes from a clipping that her mother had pinned to her father's obituary and pressed in her Bible: Those who have passed from this world die only when we, whom they loved, forget them.

To me—and to my brother and sister, I suspect—our grandparents still live.

We don't just build legacies for our children, of course. The best teachers leave legacies that span generations. The retiree who devotes his free afternoons to working with children at the Boys' and Girls' Club is building a legacy.

There's one thing about all of those legacies. They are not the results of a grand plan. They are the residue of all that we do.

A Din, Then Silence

May 2003

QUIET RETURNED TO our little corner of the lake on Monday morning. Ordinarily, the tranquility is something that I embrace, but on this day it seemed unnatural.

Shortly after sunrise, we waved goodbye to our son, our daughter-in-law and our grandson and to the last of the house guests who had come to spend time with them.

For a week and a half, the house had been filled with adults and children. Now, with my wife departed for work, there was only me and Hendry, the inside cat, and the yellow cat, who is not allowed to come inside.

I spent a good part of the day thinking about children. Those of us who are parents know that our children are always our children, no matter how old they are. And, if we are lucky, our children, no matter how old they are, still think that our homes are their homes, too, no matter how infrequently they are able to be there. When they do come home, it is because they want to, not because of some sense of duty.

From the time he was old enough to have playmates in the

neighborhood, Jeff, our older son, thought he ought to bring friends home with him, and he assumed that they would be welcomed. We liked knowing who his friends were, so his friends indeed were welcome, even if it meant that there was likely to be a kid in our kitchen at 7 o'clock in the morning.

After he left home for college, marriage and a career, he still liked to invite friends to visit. By then he asked if it was okay. The few times that it wasn't didn't discourage him from asking at other times.

So when he found that he and his family could spend some time with us as they moved from Washington, D.C., to Phoenix, Ariz., he called to ask if he could invite others to come, too. They included friends at various Air Force bases and his college roommate.

Of course it was okay.

So, for a week and a half the daily routine—and decibel level—at our house was dramatically altered.

Most of the couples had visited at one time or another, and it was interesting to see the changes. A few years ago, a gathering was almost non-stop activity. Now they have children—and more on the way—and there was a lull in the afternoon as the children (and some of the grownups) were put down for naps. Almost every room that could be closed off had a sleeping child in it.

I can still tell how tall the children were by the handprints that I haven't yet wiped off the glass in the doors.

It wasn't just our routine that was interrupted. Hendry the cat spent a good deal more time outside than she usually does, and when she was inside, she sought refuge under various pieces of furniture to avoid being seen by small children. The yellow cat, which I thought might disappear after encountering our son's dog, instead intimidated the dog and continued to have his morning and evening meals on the side deck, ignoring the comings and goings.

On Monday, Hendry spent the day curled up in a chair, and the yellow cat dozed on the doormat. I wandered around the quiet house, restoring order.

Folks often talk of being glad to see the headlights when guests come and glad to see the taillights when they leave. To some extent that's true. But give me a few days to recover and I'll look forward to seeing the headlights again.

While You're Commuting

March 2005

IN THE SMALL towns where we lived when I was a kid, many men went home for lunch. Some went home every day, others a few times a week. It was easy for them to go home, because the places where they lived were within walking distance—or at most a five- or six-minute drive—from where they worked.

In the summer, the stores closed on Wednesday afternoons (some places in small towns still do), and year round, most businesses seemed to close around 5 or 5:30. (I wonder whether the tradition of 6 p.m. being time for the news was established because most people were home from work by then).

On the farms, of course, the men ate lunch—only it was really dinner—at home almost every day.

We did not live in any large cities when I was a kid, but I suspect that the distance to and from work was not terribly far in most large cities.

This short trip down memory lane was spurred by a spate of newspaper and magazine articles about commuting recently.

BusinessWeek magazine reported that the number of "extreme

157

commuters"—people who spend at least a month of their lives each year just going to and from work—has jumped 95 percent (to 3.4 million workers) since 1990. And the numbers are predicted to grow.

Although we identify long commutes with places like New York, Washington and Los Angeles, most of us have acquaintances who make long commutes daily. I know people who commute from Dadeville to Birmingham and from Lanett to Wetumpka, a distance of about 90 miles..

People in Alabama commute for the same reasons that people do in other areas: they're looking for what we think of as the good life: quality schools, affordable homes, safe neighborhoods. They're willing to trade their time for them. The evidence is mostly anecdotal, but Auburn's good public schools seem to have attracted a lot of people who are willing to drive to Montgomery or Columbus, Ga., to go to work every day.

Commuting doesn't mean just driving anymore; it involves a host of other things, which might not be a good thing. The National Highway Traffic Safety Administration just released a survey that showed 8 percent of drivers (that's 1.2 million people) were using cell phones during daylight hours last year, a 50 percent increase since 2002.

Commuters don't just drive and talk, either. They finish dressing, they listen to books, they eat. It's a sign of how common taking meals behind the wheel has become when Campbell's Soup comes in handy containers that you can grip while you're driving.

And more than once I've seen a driver on the interstate with paperwork or a folded newspaper propped against the steering wheel.

Although some commuters say they value their private time (more than 80 percent of Alabama commuters ride alone, according to an article in USA Today), there are experts who claim that commuters can experience as much stress as a fighter pilot or a riot policeman. One expert has identified a syndrome called "commuter amnesia" in which stress causes people to forget large parts of their journey.

I am not citing all of this to call for a return to the "good old days," which never really were as good as we like to recall.

Times have changed, and our lives have changed with them. Some of us have life thrust upon us, but most make choices. We've chosen to swap a hunk of our time for those things that we think are important.

I sometimes wonder, though, whether we get so accustomed to the way things are that we don't question whether the trade is still a good one. As my wife's great aunt used to observe, "You'd get used to hanging if it didn't kill you."

Back in the '60s John Lennon famously observed that "life is what happens to you while you're making other plans."

Or perhaps while you're commuting.

Yellow Cat and the Vet

May 2004

I DON'T KNOW yet how this story is going to turn out.

The Yellow Cat and I had a disagreement about whether he should go to the veterinarian. I had to force the issue.

The Yellow Cat is not our cat, but I am the cat's person. He does not have a name—other than Yellow Cat—because giving him a name would be symbolic of ownership.

It took some time for us to reach our relationship, which has become somewhat strained by our current disagreement. He usually appears at the side door morning and night, peering through the glass until I put his food dish out.

At one point last year he disappeared for weeks, and I thought he was gone for good. He returned one evening as abruptly as he disappeared. I saw him sitting at the end of the deck as if waiting for dinner. When I took his dish out, he forgot his inhibitions and rubbed against my leg as if he were really pleased to see me.

Since then he has settled in, though he's not allowed inside. His coat is sleek and his ribs no longer stick out. In fact, he is something of a tub. He rubs against my leg and occasionally lets me scratch his ears. Sometimes I pick him up, but he doesn't like to be held for long.

He was lolling in the sun on the side deck the other day and I noticed an open wound on his hip. I guessed that it was an abscess.

I asked my wife to bring the cat carrier out after I had the cat in hand. I had put on a pair of work gloves and picked the cat up from the bench. My wife came out with the carrier.

The Yellow Cat wanted no part of it. In an instant he twisted out of my hands and bounded over the railing. A cat that does not wish to be held is pretty good at not being held for long.

He kept his distance the rest of the day.

I don't know whether he was forgetful or forgiving, but he appeared for breakfast the next morning. As he was eating, I tried to wrap a beach towel around him. My determination was no match for his.

I thought he might take off for parts unknown, but he hung around, regarding me warily and keeping an escape path clear.

I thought I was going to have to borrow a Havahart trap from Dr. John Caldwell, our veterinarian, although I was not sanguine about it working. The Yellow Cat didn't survive on his own by being careless.

When I returned home Wednesday afternoon, the Yellow Cat was taking the sun on the settee on the side deck. I scratched his ears, and he didn't flinch. I went inside and put on a jacket to try to protect me from scratches. I left the door open. The cat let me pick him up and appeared only mildly apprehensive when I took him into the house.

He put up only token resistance when I put him in the carrier, and he uttered not a meow as I drove him to our vet's office.

The office had closed, but fortunately Dr. Caldwell was still there. When I left, the cat was eating from a dish of food laced with antibiotics.

What I don't know is whether he will stick around when I bring him back from his unwanted imprisonment.

The Yellow Cat doesn't realize that my intentions are good.

Sometimes it's hard to understand that somebody is trying to help you, especially if you're not used to it.

————

An update on Yellow Cat: YC is home after staying for several days at the veterinarian's office. And Yellow Cat is staying in the house, to the chagrin of my wife and Hendry, the indoor cat. Yellow Cat doesn't seem thrilled about it either.

We thought Yellow Cat was a female, but the vet tells us it's a neutered male. He is confined to a small part of the house until all of the antibiotics are gone and the wound, which turned out to be a bite, is healed. Meanwhile he is wearing a shield around his neck to keep him from biting at the wound. It gives him the appearance of one of those drawings you see of Elizabethan women in dresses with stiff, circular collars, as he gazes wistfully through the glass panes of the hall door.

Sloth on a Rainy Day

June 2005

THE TUESDAY AFTER Memorial Day was gray and rainy at the lake. It was a perfect time for an experiment in doing nothing in particular. Actually, I thought of it as sloth.

I'd just completed all of my projects that had immediate deadlines, and although there's no shortage of items on my personal and professional to-do lists, nothing bad would happen if I didn't whittle away at any of them for a day. One of the benefits of being retired or semi-retired is that you can give yourself permission to do —or not do—things.

So after I kissed my wife goodbye—she's self-employed and has a demanding boss—I made the short trip into town for breakfast with the usual suspects, always an enjoyable hour. The sky opened up before I got home, and I determined not to go out again.

Sloth, I thought, would require me to stay out of my home office—too much potential work in there—and to leave the television turned off. I weakened briefly to check the e-mail to make certain there was nothing that absolutely demanded attention.

I wasn't quite sure what to do with myself. I'm so accustomed to being directed by a to-do list that charting a day of "nothing in particular" was a challenge.

So I took all 51 CDs out of the player. They'd been put in randomly over time, and I had been meaning to sort them out. I put them back in, writing down the slot each one occupied so that I could actually play something I wanted to hear.

A mystery novel by Alabama writer Mike Stewart was on the table beside my chair in the little reading alcove off our bedroom. I had started it several months ago but had made little headway, reading only a few pages on the odd evening. I rarely read in the daytime; that same inchoate guilt that made me think that I had to finish any book I started also discourages reading, especially fiction, during the daytime when I ought to be doing something.

I removed Hendry the cat—an unabashed master of sloth—from my chair and sat reading. The rain on the roof was hypnotic. Soon the recliner was fully extended and my eyes were closed. Hendry, who had stalked out of the room when she was evicted from the chair, has the uncanny ability to detect a horizontal body from a great distance, and I had a vague awareness of her stretched out on my chest. It is not that Hendry loves me; it is that she loves a soft, warm place.

It rained and we snoozed.

When I eased back into consciousness, it was lunchtime. I turned the television set on briefly while I consumed a piece of cold chicken, but my resolve asserted itself and I clicked it off.

Despite the clouds and rain, the temperature was comfortable, and I sat with my book on the screened porch overlooking the water. There were no boats, no sounds except rain on the leaves and the drip of water from the eaves onto the deck.

I read until tea time. When I was a kid, I could get lost in a book for hours, but it had been a long, long time since I'd read for so long at a stretch. After tea, I curled up in a chair in the living room and read until I turned the last page. It had taken two or three months to read the first 100 pages or so; the remainder of the 416 pages had taken only a few hours.

When I'd finished, I caved in and turned on the local news on television. Back to the real world.

When they were younger, our two sons—now grown and busy —used to tease about dad wanting to install a sprinkler system and find a cure for cancer before breakfast.

I think they'd be proud of me.

Fatigue Hits the Common Good

February 2005

I'VE BEEN SOMEWHAT slack about picking up litter this winter.

Some time ago I took it upon myself to try to keep a stretch of road near our house from becoming a garbage dump. But in recent months it has been too cold, too wet, and too busy. All of those are plausible excuses; all of them contain at least some element of truth.

I drive along that road almost every day, and through much of the winter there did not seem to be many aluminum cans, paper and plastic bags, drink cups, cigarette packages and the sundry other items that find their way onto the roadside. I kept thinking that I'd get out and pick up the following week.

Finally, the accumulation was so noticeable that my conscience —abetted by a bright, spring-like day—spurred me to action. It did not take long to fill a large trash bag.

I wasn't the only one that the weather energized. Later in the afternoon I saw two women collecting litter on another road. Plastic grocery bags, filled and neatly tied, marked their progress.

The next morning there was a cardboard box beside my road, its contents strewn. By afternoon, though, box and contents were

YELLOW CAT, HENDRY & ME

gone. It helps to know that there are other people who care how our community looks.

I ordinarily walk for exercise, so picking up litter isn't that much extra effort, and it helps keep the moving parts working. And I, like many others who pick up after our fellow citizens, find the accumulation of roadside trash more offensive than they do.

Ultimately, though, picking up litter—like so many other volunteer efforts, is something that makes the community better, something for the common good.

The people who run charities talk about donor fatigue. After the outpouring of aid for the victims of the tsunami, many agency heads are worried that their customary donors will be tapped out.

I think volunteers suffer from fatigue, too, whether they are part of an organized effort or have just taken some task on for themselves. That's especially true in small communities where the same people are called on for every kind of effort until they just burn out.

At bottom, I suspect that I took leave from my litter collecting just because I was tired of doing it.

There are no penalties when volunteers quit volunteering. There's no knock on the door summoning them to get back to the effort.

So, the need remains, even if the effort evaporates.

That may be why we institutionalized so many activities that contributed to what a majority of people considered to be the common good. (Old age assistance is an example. So is the food stamp program.) We thought we were all in the same boat and that we all ought to pull on the oars. If we didn't want to make the commitment to do it ourselves, we were willing to pay taxes to try to ensure that the need was met.

I don't recall people talking a lot about the common good, even when they believed that there was such a thing.

Efforts to define and work toward the common good date back at least to the Greek philosophers. The common good seems to be a part of the social gospel, although some Christians see working for the common good as a mandate for collective action and others see it as a matter of individual conscience.

In this country, we champion individualism, and there has always been a tension between accepting a common good and individual rights. As people and groups have asserted their own identities and values, the balance has shifted, and we find less agreement on what constitutes the common good.

Instead of all pulling on the same oar, we are more inclined to paddle our own boats.

I am not sure whether we should celebrate the growth of individuality or mourn the demise of community. Perhaps a little of both.

Broken Things, Part II

February 2005

I FINALLY FINISHED patching the hole that dunderhead made when he stepped through the ceiling of the front bedroom while getting the Christmas decorations out of the attic.

Not Christmas 2004. Christmas 2003.

That is also the last time that I tried to get an early start on Christmas decorating. Just as people always seem to break a leg on what was to be the last ski run of the day, I broke the ceiling as I was fetching the last box from the dark recesses of the attic.

When I lost my balance and felt my foot shoot into space, I knew something bad was about to happen. A ceiling joist caught most of my body, and the only thing broken was the drywall. Taking a leaf from my son the optimist's book, I concluded that I was lucky that my entire body hadn't hurtled into the room below.

In the front bedroom, the evidence of my misadventure was more than a little obvious. I cut away the broken drywall that was hanging down and vacuumed up the mess. I could feel the warm air from the bedroom being sucked up into the attic.

Fortunately, I keep a supply of duct tape on hand, so I taped a black plastic garbage bag over the hole. The thin bag shivered as the rising warm air tried to push through it.

That bedroom is one we use for guests, and days pass without either of us going into it. Chances were that my wife wouldn't have noticed the damage right away, but we had company coming. I knew that I couldn't get the ceiling fixed before then, so I pointed out the damage and emphasized how lucky I was that I hadn't incurred a medical bill.

Our house guest had the good grace to mention the unusual ceiling only in passing.

I grew up in a time and place in which you didn't hire someone to do what you could do yourself—it was a matter of pride and money—and we all thought we could do just about anything.

My wife has been trying to persuade me for years that there are times when it is a good idea to pay someone to do something. I have had enough experience with drywall to know that I need at least twice as much time and twice as much compound as a pro would, so it seemed a good time to trust her judgment

A painter who had done work for us said he'd take care of the job. A couple of weeks passed before he showed up, but in a short time he'd trimmed the hole, cut and installed a patch to fit it and applied tape and compound. He'd stop back by in a few days to apply a second coat, he said. Altogether the repair would require two or three trips.

That was roughly a year ago, and I haven't seen the painter since. Fixing my ceiling was a little job, and he had bigger and more profitable things to do.

It became easy to ignore the piece of bare drywall, and the guests who used the room have either had the good manners not to mention it or were too busy looking at the lake to notice.

That unfinished job gave me some insight into why people put up with dented autos and why litter remains by the roadside. We just get so accustomed to things as they are that we don't notice them anymore.

I was infused with a fresh burst of energy after recovering from a virus in January, and I decided to finish the job myself. After I moved the furniture out of the room, it took a few hours, spread over three or four days, to finish the job and spray the patch with texture to blend in with the rest of the ceiling. Of course I had to paint the entire ceiling to make everything match.

Dealing with the job offered another insight: If you make a big enough mess, you can probably get someone else to fix it. Make a small mess and you'll probably have to fix it yourself.

I realized that since the bedroom is empty, I might as well rent a carpet cleaner. And polish the brass bed.

Which validates another truism: one thing leads to another.

Grabbing Magic Moments

April 2005

A FEW BUDS on the wild azaleas in the sunniest spot on our half hill opened a couple of Saturdays ago. By the next day, a few more had opened, and by Monday, they were in their full glory.

They were followed by those in the shadier spots. Now the dogwoods have joined them, and the oak leaf hydrangeas are putting out their tender green leaves.

That is the way spring arrives, first with a few hints, like the swelling of the azalea buds, and then with a rush.

And there are the fire flies.

For once, Day Light Saving Time seemed to arrive at the right moment.

On the Monday after we pushed the time forward, my wife arrived home from her office before dark. She had brought work home with her, and I still had several hours' worth of things to do.

But it was still daylight, and although a few clouds had drifted in, it remained one of those inviting spring days when the evening brings a touch of coolness to the air.

Work could wait, at least for a little while.

We grabbed our jackets and hurried down to the pontoon boat. Never mind the pollen coating the seats. We cranked the engine and cast off. Our only destination was the outdoors.

Down the way, we spotted lights on in the cabin of friends who are usually at the lake only on the weekends. We eased up to their dock and found that Tom was home. We coaxed him away from the work that he was doing.

We eased along, the motor turning so quietly that we could converse in normal tones. The evening invited a slower pace.

Over beyond Smith Mountain, the last light of the sun painted a red streak on the clouds, and then it was gone. Lights glimmered along the shore.

Lake Martin is a big lake, some 750 miles of shoreline and 40,000 acres of water. It's a good bet that somewhere on the lake others were celebrating a real spring evening, but in our little corner of the lake, we were alone.

We dropped Tom off at his dock and puttered slowly back around the point.

We hadn't left any lights on, and our house loomed darkly above the water. We picked up the dock in the glow of the navigation lights and tied up

From the dock we looked up at the dark bulk of the house and at the silhouettes of the still bare trees and at the lighter sky behind them.

It was as if we had entered a magic show.

There were fireflies everywhere, too numerous to count. Some were above the roof and others flitted through the trees.

Scientists tell us that there are 136 species of fireflies, all of them carnivorous members of the beetle family. Those fireflies we see in the air are males flashing signals for potential mates that are on or near the ground. The females signal back, and eventually the fireflies pair up. It's sort of an aerial singles bar.

Regardless of what the scientists call it, though, I call it magic, and we paused to take it all in.

Work awaited—work always seems to be waiting—but it could wait a little longer. Magic moments pass, and there are times when there is nothing more important than stopping to appreciate the moment.

Geezers, Callow Youth, Stereotypes

April 2005

THE HEADLINE LEAPT out at me: 60-year-old-man will hike 460 miles on Appalachian (Trail).

Implicit in that headline was amazement that someone so old would actually undertake something so physical.

"Listen, buddy," I wanted to say to the headline writer. "Considering the epidemic of obesity among the younger set, there probably are as many of us over 60 capable of making the hike as there are under 30."

The story didn't have quite the gee-whiz focus as the headline. It pointed out that the subject of the story had been training for his adventure, which is the same thing someone under 30 should do before setting out on a long hike.

Still, the story was pegged on the age of the hiker, and I couldn't help wondering whether the plans of a 59-year-old to hike the Appalachian Trail would have been considered newsworthy,

Of course, 30 or 35 years ago, I wouldn't have found any reason to comment on the headline; I might have even written it myself.

When I graduated from college, I took a job in an area of

Florida thick with retirees. The site of an old geezer on the beach wearing a pith helmet, plaid shorts and black socks sent us 20-somethings into stitches of laughter. Didn't they realize how ridiculous they looked? Ah, the arrogance of youth.

It is something of a shock to realize that some of those "geezers" were no older than I am now. And it is oddly comforting to realize, too, that they were not in the least concerned about what we young whippersnappers thought.

I have found that old age is a moving target, changing as we ourselves get older. I've got a few years on that Appalachian hiker, and my present definition of old age is always at least 10 years older than I am.

Despite the fact that our population is getting older—the percentage of the United States population over 65 will increase from 12 percent today to about 20 percent by 2030—there remains the casual assumption that people beyond a certain age are mentally and physically marginal.

It will be interesting to see whether the Baby Boomers can dispel some of the stereotypes. Meanwhile, those of us who are, shall we say, in our mature years, face some contradictions.

We don't want to be treated as being different in the way that older people were treated in early generations. We want to be treated as adults, but we really don't want our restaurant server—to use the more politically correct term—to treat us with a breezy casualness that suggests he or she wants to be our best friend. (Of course, I didn't care for that even when I was a lot closer to the server's age.)

Another contradiction: We keep hearing discussion of raising the retirement age to help preserve Social Security while some companies continue to push older workers out the door. The older workers, who usually also are the most highly paid, get the message that they just can't cut it anymore. (When the older workers finally leave, though, they are often replaced with younger workers whose salaries are considerably less. The U.S. Supreme Court in a ruling March 30 made it easier for older workers to sue for age discrimination.)

If the younger generation is guilty of stereotyping, though, the older generation doesn't get off Scot free.

I think we need to try to reach an understanding with the younger generation: Don't condescend to me by assuming that my energy and mental powers are on some inexorable downward slide, and I won't condescendingly assume that you are too young to have any experience or judgment that is worthwhile.

In the meantime, that article has gotten me to thinking about having a go at the Appalachian Trail. I might get an even bigger headline.

A Checkup for Hendry

May 2005

I MADE THE MISTAKE of calling the veterinarian's office to schedule Hendry's annual checkup and vaccinations while she was curled up in her chair near my desk, her usual place when I am working in my office. She takes her supervisory role seriously.

We'd received cards from the vet's office reminding us that Hendry and Yellow Cat were due for their annual visit.

Hendry is the indoor cat that goes outdoors occasionally, usually when one of us goes out.

Yellow Cat—the card from the vet referred to him as Big Yellow Cat, an accurate description—does not belong to us or to anyone else, but he has selected me as his guardian. Yellow Cat—a description when he was a bedraggled stray and later a name of sorts when he decided that our house was home—does not come inside because Hendry and my wife prefer it that way.

I scheduled Hendry's checkup for that afternoon. I didn't notice that Hendry had followed me down the stairs and was lurking right behind me when I opened the front door for a moment. Hendry bolted out.

No worry, I thought, she'll want to come in before it's time to go to the vet. At no point during the day did she come anywhere near the door. Instead, she lounged on the bench by the back deck. She perched on the path along the side of the house. She sat in the driveway keeping an eye on the Yellow Cat.

As the time for the appointment approached, I went to the door and called her. She looked at me and pretended that I must be calling some other creature. I approached slowly. She retreated. I followed her along the path, under the front deck—it is well off the ground—and out again. She remained just out of reach in this low speed chase.

Yellow Cat sat in the driveway watching with some interest.

I broke off my fruitless pursuit of Hendry. If Hendry didn't want to be caught, she wouldn't be.

Yellow Cat needed to go to the vet, too, I reasoned, and it wouldn't matter which cat had the first visit.

I walked slowly toward Yellow Cat, speaking softly. Yellow Cat didn't wish to participate. Following Hendry's example, he ambled down the drive just quickly enough to stay ahead of me. I speeded up and he scrambled down the embankment and sat looking up at me, somewhat smugly, I thought.

I started down the bank. Yellow Cat disappeared into the culvert that runs under the driveway.

I am stubborn, but I recognize defeat. I went inside to cancel the appointment. Through the window, though, I saw Hendry lolling on the railing of the front deck.

I eased out of the door, leaving it open. I circled widely until I was between her and the steps. The deck is too far off the ground for her to jump. She sensed my intention, made a feint toward the steps, and darted into the house.

Hendry got her shots after all.

It was Yellow Cat's turn.

Every morning, Yellow Cat is staring hopefully through the door, waiting for breakfast. He is there in the evening, too. After living a life of uncertainty, Yellow Cat likes the security of having food available on demand.

Yellow Cat harbors some residual suspicion of humans at all times. After watching Hendry being carried away in a carrier, he made sure there was an escape route clear when he came to his dish.

After a couple of weeks, though, appetite overcame caution, and I grabbed him while his head was buried in the food dish.

Next time, I'll make certain that Hendry's not listening when I talk to the vet. And I'll snare Yellow Cat first.

The cats and I both are just as happy that we only have to do this once a year.

Playing for Time

May 2005

FEELING BELEAGUERED by the demands I have created for myself, I abandoned them the other morning to take a brief stroll.

After spending an entire career in a profession—or craft—in which time is always important and in short supply, I began the next phase of my life—it's hard to call it retirement—by putting my Palm Pilot, a graphic description, in a desk drawer.

Instead of measuring my life in minutes and hours, I thought, I could simply note the few commitments I expected to make on the calendar.

I cannot explain where my plan failed except to acknowledge that old habits die hard. It was not long before I had gotten involved with a multitude of personal and civic projects that must have deadlines if they are to get done. The Palm Pilot is now on top of my desk, and I always seem to have a notebook with me. And still I get behind.

The side of me that whines, "I'm way too busy" gets no sympathy from the side that says, "And whose fault is that?"

So on this particular morning I deserted the field of internal conflict and slipped out the door.

The morning was still cool, and the rain of the day before had washed the sky so that it was clean and deep.

The county road department had not begun mowing the right of way yet, and the roadside was abundant with wild flowers, most of which I cannot name. The wet spring that turned the roadside into a garden also brought lush growth to the woods. The dogwoods and the wild azaleas seemed to last far longer than they usually do. Along my route a lone dogwood was finally shedding its blossoms, petal by petal.

There were tiny berries on the blueberry bushes along the way. The birds and other wildlife will get most of them, but I will stop to gather a handful when they get ripe. There were white blossoms on the blackberry bushes at the edge of the woods. The sight of them summoned a reminder of my first encounter with chiggers, or red bugs as we called them then.

The morning rush, if you could call it that, had passed, and there was only an occasional automobile or truck to momentarily drown out the sounds of nature. The breeze occasionally brought the ring of hammers where someone was working on a house, but it was the birds that dominated the sound track. A bird that I could not see was singing endlessly "purty, purty, purty." I don't know whether he was referring to himself or the day at hand. In either case, the description seemed appropriate.

A dog lying in a yard along the way was enjoying the morning in his own way. As I passed, he raised his head and gave a perfunctory bark. Another dog sitting farther up the driveway was a little more vocal, but he decided that it wasn't worth the trouble to actually get up, and when I was out of sight they lapsed into silence.

The way eventually led home and to the duties I had temporarily abandoned; I had not intended to walk quite so far, but my feet had set their own direction without my conscious input.

None of the chores had gone away while I was out for a stroll, but they didn't look quite so big.

And I realized that I had not looked at my watch during the entire time I was out.

The Bus Doesn't Stop Here

July 2005

FROM ABBEVILLE TO York, Alabama small towns are trying to find ways to cope with Greyhound Bus Lines' decision to close its stations in 39 cities.

Many of those small towns are already isolated from urban Alabama. Now they are cut off even further. While thousands of us are able to cruise the information superhighway, many small town residents can't take a real highway to the next town.

Greyhound isn't to be blamed for eliminating routes where it was not making money. Progress means that many people who used to ride buses haven't been on one for years. They have more convenient means of transportation.

Progress has been uneven, though, and it is easy to forget that there are still people who don't have automobiles or who cannot drive for one reason or another.

It's hard enough to get by without a personal vehicle, even if you live in a city. It's even more difficult in the smaller towns where commerce has dried up and the doctors have moved away.

There are towns like that scattered all over the landscape, towns that once bustled on Saturday when country people came early and spent their day shopping and catching up on visiting.

The small town retail stores are mostly gone now, replaced by pawn shops, tanning parlors and video rental businesses. Store windows on once thriving main streets are boarded over and trees grow out of rain gutters on the sides of buildings.

Wal-Mart, good roads and the widespread ownership of automobiles dealt a body blow to the small towns. The suspension of bus service will make it even harder for some people to stay in them.

Even when the small towns thrived, there were reasons to go to other cities. As those towns have offered less in the way of shopping and services, such as medical care, there is even more need to be able to reach a larger city.

I haven't ridden a bus in decades, but it was always nice to know that they were available to fall back on.

When I was a kid in small town Louisiana, my mother often put me on a bus to ride the 30 or 40 miles to visit my grandparents. The trip was an adventure as the bus made its way from one small town to another, picking up or dropping off passengers and sometimes packages. Occasionally the stop was a real bus station, but often it was just a filling station. The world is a more dangerous place now, and most parents wouldn't dream of putting their child on a bus.

I guess most college students have cars now, but there was a time when the bus was the way that many of them got home for the holidays.

Even after I graduated from college, my old car wasn't always running, and on my day off I would take a bus from St. Petersburg, Fla., to Daytona Beach where my fiancée worked. The bus seemed to zigzag across every small town in the middle part of the state, and sometimes my time on the bus seemed to be as long as my time with my girl. In fact, one of those trips to Daytona Beach may have been my last time on a bus.

Even in a small town, you once could go to the bus station or filling station and buy a ticket that connected you to a wider world.

Mobility was simply the price of a bus ticket, but having ticket money doesn't make any difference if the bus doesn't stop in your town.

Things You Don't Outgrow

August 2005

WE WENT TO a child's birthday party on a recent Saturday. I was glad I didn't miss it. Of course you don't miss your grandchildren's birthdays if you are anywhere near, even though your presence is noted only in passing by the honoree.

All birthdays are special, of course, but this party tugged a few special strings.

Our younger son's family lives in Montgomery, and the party was for the youngest of their three daughters, who was turning four. Even though I occasionally grumble at being a useless appendage at such events, the children grow and change so quickly that it's difficult to turn down an opportunity to see them. Everyone is so scheduled these days that sometimes an hour's distance might as well be half a continent.

Our daughter-in-law is a creative party planner, and this one was at the city park in Old Alabama Town in Montgomery. There is a great new playground for children, and the park is fenced, so it's easier to keep an eye on everyone.

The party had a western theme, so there were cowboy hats,

187

badges and water pistols for all of the kids.

What made it special for us was that some of the children running around were first cousins. Our older son and his wife and two children will be at Maxwell Air Force Base in Montgomery for nearly a year, so for the first time our children and grandchildren are all in the same town.

Seeing the cousins together sent me on a nostalgia trip. I grew up with cousins all around. We played, we thought up things to do, we fought and we defended each other, and we got into trouble together. We depended on our grandmother to be a shield for us.

We see each other too seldom now—time and distance separate us—but when we are together what we talk about most often are the things we got in trouble for.

Our two boys did not have cousins nearby, but they were close enough in age to have friends in common, and they thought up things to do, fought, defended each other, and got into trouble together.

And they kept their lips as tightly zipped as any Mafioso. When they and we are together, they recall the things they got in trouble for. Whatever statute of limitations there might have been has long since expired, so they feel free to talk about the things that they'd have been in trouble for, if only we had caught them at the time.

I'm sure the list would have been longer if a few cousins had joined the mix.

Cousins are among life's blessings—at least most of the time. As I watched the children playing, I hoped that by the time our son's assignment at Maxwell ends, the children will have the opportunity to build some memories that they will recall fondly later. They're a little young to get in much trouble, and I'm pretty sure their grandmother will cover for them.

As satisfying as it was to watch the children at play on Saturday, though, perhaps the best part was seeing our two grown sons chasing each other with water pistols, too. There are some things, thank goodness, that you don't outgrow.

Play's the Thing

March 2008

I AM TRYING to learn to play again; I knew how as a child and as a young adult.

At some point, though, play for its own sake faded. If I weren't working on the job, I was working on some kind of project, either from my list of things to do or in a community effort. These are the kinds of things that have a goal and a result to be measured.

I don't want to stop doing those things; they offer rewards of their own. I am learning, though, that not every moment has to be programmed and accounted for.

An observation by Eric Hoffer, the longshoreman/philosopher, bolsters my case: "Take away play, fancies, and luxuries, and you will turn man into a dull, sluggish creature, barely energetic enough to obtain a bare subsistence. A society becomes stagnant when its people are too rational or too serious to be tempted by baubles."

That sounds a little more profound than "all work and no play makes Jack a dull boy."

So it was that recently I found myself with two friends who are former colleagues with nothing on our agenda except to play.

190

It was a postcard spring day, one of those that begins cool enough to call for a light jacket and turns to shirt-sleeve comfort. A breeze added freshness to the air.

In this lovely setting I was trying to make a little white ball bend to my will.

I took a mighty swing and the little ball popped into the air and landed a few feet away.

It did not much matter. Guys need to have an excuse to spend the day just hanging out, and our excuse was golf.

It had been a long time since I had been on a golf course. I took golf—took is more accurate than learned—in phys ed in college; in those days, phys ed was required for most college students.

I didn't have a natural talent for the game, but I enjoyed it, and for a year or so after college, I played with a buddy of mine on a flat public course in Florida where there wasn't much difference between the fairway and the rough.

When the first of our children came along, I put the clubs away and eventually sold them at a garage sale.

I didn't really think about golf again until a few years ago when I shared office space with a devoted golfer.

On Mondays, Jim would talk about the beautiful course he had played on the weekend. He was almost poetic, and before long I began itching to get out. He assured me that the equipment was a lot better than it had been when I last played, and he lent me a few old clubs to prove it. I signed up for a group golf class at Auburn University in Montgomery's continuing education program.

Then the aggravation of a long-time back problem put an end to any thoughts about taking up the game again (and maybe I didn't want to spend time in a nonproductive activity).

Not long ago, though, I took the borrowed clubs to the driving range and found that I could swing a club without making my back hurt. Jim was right. Modern clubs are better. I am not.

My wife listened for a long time to my vague talk about playing. So she gave me a set of clubs for my birthday; it was time to put up or shut up.

Al, another former colleague, who had played at golf before giving it up in frustration, was lured back by Jim's eloquence.

So the three of us met in Selma and played on a picturesque public course a few miles out of town.

Golf was a great excuse for hanging out.

And I hit just enough good shots to make me want to go again.

There's another observation from Hoffer that I will pin on the wall as a reminder if I begin feeling guilty about just going out and playing: "Man was shaped less by what he had to do than by what he did in playful moments. It is the child in man that is the source of his uniqueness and creativeness, and the playground is the optimal milieu for the unfolding of his capacities."

Death Comes to the Yellow Cat

Spring 2008

ALMOST EVERY MORNING, I come down the stairs and look toward the door. Yellow Cat should be there, staring patiently through the glass, head cocked to one side, waiting for breakfast to be served. He should be there in the evening, too, sitting on the stoop and staring into the darkness as if something were out there just beyond the pool of light.

Yellow Cat is not there because he died, suddenly and unexpectedly, on a raw March morning, and I have not yet absorbed that reality.

Yellow Cat was not my cat; in fact, he was no one's cat, although I do not know whether that was by his choice or whether someone abandoned him. Over the past four years, though, we had achieved an understanding: I would provide food and water and take him to the vet for shots or to be patched up when he occasionally got wounded by some more aggressive creature. In exchange, he would decorate the porch railing or the deck or the driveway, lolling in the sun or curled up into a ball on the bench.

On the Wednesday morning that he died, Yellow Cat was at the side door as was his habit, waiting patiently.

I filled his dish—it had been licked clean, which meant that a coon or possum had wandered by; Yellow Cat always left a few crumbs.

A couple of hours later, I went to put some things in the car preparatory to taking my wife to Birmingham for a medical appointment. Yellow Cat was sprawled on the side deck, looking very much as he did when he stretched out in a warm, sunny spot. The day, however, was cold and windy, and ordinarily he would have taken shelter under the tea olive bush at corner of the house.

He was dead, peacefully dead, as if the end had come by surprise, and I would like to think, painlessly. There were no marks on him, not even any signs of discomfort. It must have happened not long before I found him, because rigor had not yet set in. When animals know that they are dying, they often seek a secluded spot to pass away. Yellow Cat apparently didn't have that warning, and I'm glad, because if he had simply disappeared, I would always have wondered what happened to him.

I covered him to keep the buzzards or other animals from getting to him, and when we got home I buried him on the hillside overlooking the lake. My wife donated flowers from a bouquet that someone had sent her.

The next day, I called our veterinarian to tell him about Yellow Cat's death and to ask whether I should be concerned about the health of the indoor cat. The circumstances of death didn't yield a ready explanation, and he asked me to remove Yellow Cat from his hillside so he could be sent to the veterinary school at Auburn for a post-mortem.

So I carefully exhumed him from his hillside and took him to the vet.

I said goodbye to Yellow Cat for a second time.

A few weeks later, the vet called me with the autopsy report.

Yellow Cat died of a heart attack. We never knew how old he was, and a heart attack was a far easier death than the renal failure that claims so many older cats. And I would like to think that his last years were good ones for him.

Even so, I waited until May to erase the last physical sign of Yellow Cat's presence in our lives with a few strokes of a paintbrush. After he died in March, I put away the little house I'd built for him —one that he seldom deigned to use, no matter how cold the weather—and discarded his food and water dishes.

But I left the scars on the corner board at the top of the steps leading from the side deck to the alcove just outside the door. Yellow Cat was a big guy, and he liked to stretch full length against the corner board and drag his claws down the soft cedar. I covered the scars with gray stain any number of times. It would last for a while, but sooner or later he felt the urge to stretch and etch into the wood the sign that this was his home.

The scratches on the corner board didn't mean anything to anyone except me. And I realized that it wasn't necessary to preserve the claw marks to preserve the memory that resides somewhere in my mind.

And, early in the morning, I still look toward the door, halfway expecting to see Yellow Cat there looking back at me.

Making Do

April 2009

Use it up, wear it out, make it do or do without.
Yankee Proverb

THE PROVERB CAME to mind not long ago as I read a newspaper article reporting that in this trying economy more people are having their clothing mended and shoes resoled, using the public library instead of buying on Amazon, and preparing more meals at home instead of eating out.

It came to mind again as I was wheeling the garbage can to the street. It was nearly full, despite the fact that only my wife and I live at home, and we recycle newspapers and magazines, aluminum and steel cans and cardboard. We save our plastic grocery bags for use by the food pantry.

What is it that we are throwing away? By far, the most substantial part of it is packaging. Everything seems to come in multiple layers of paper and plastic. Some of it is leftovers that got left over for too long. It is obvious that we are throwing out more than we're wearing out.

Whether you call it frugality or conservation, it is unarguable that our footprint on this planet is much larger than that of the generations that went before us.

I'm sure that the generation my grandparents belonged to didn't think of themselves as being eco-friendly, or as we say now, "green." They thought they were simply being sensible.

Certainly industries used our air and our streams as convenient dumps and didn't concern themselves with the consequences.

On a lesser level, not everything my grandparents did, such as burning household garbage in an empty oil drum and then burying what remained in an old gravel pit, was particularly earth friendly. But on the whole, they made far fewer demands on the planet's resources than we do.

We buy paper towels by the case; my grandmother wiped the kitchen counter with a cloth from a 25-pound bag of flour.

Many in our generation and even more in the one following us buy bottled water. When my grandfather went to the field, he carried his drinking water, which came from the well, in a gallon syrup jug, insulated with an empty 10-pound sugar sack.

Most of the food was grown in the garden and didn't come shrink-wrapped in a Styrofoam tray. Meat purchased at the grocery store was wrapped in butcher paper instead of plastic. Far more items, from foodstuffs to hardware were sold unpackaged.

My grandfather's old Studebaker pickup truck probably was not as efficient as the engines of today's vehicles. But he drove fewer miles in a year than we do in a month.

The closets in my grandparents' house were impossibly small, but the closets and a couple of chiffarobes held everything they owned, and they did not feel compelled buy new things before the old clothes wore out.

At our house, the clothes dryer runs a good deal of the time; I can't remember when we last lived in a house that had a clothesline.

Although my grandmother eventually had an automatic washing machine, she never had a dryer and never felt the need for one.

I don't hold those days up as the ideal. Times change, and so do we. I'm pretty sure, though, that despite our consumption of a larger share of the planet's bounty, we are not really any happier than they were.

Would we be more content if we owned less, if we used less? I don't know. All that simplicity may be more attractive in the abstract.

Intellectually, I know we have all kinds of stuff that we don't really need, but as long as we have a place to put it—even if we can't remember where we put it, or sometimes even remember that we have it—simplifying will continue to be a challenge.

My efforts thus far have been limited. I've thinned my library of a fair number of books, taking them to the public library for use in one of the Friends of the Library's periodic book sales. But I have to consider a book multiple times before I admit that I'm not going to read it again or use it for reference. I've gotten rid of bags of clothing that no longer fits, things that are too big instead of too small. I want to make it expensive to regain the weight I've lost.

It was easy enough for Thoreau to preach, "Simplify, simplify, simplify."

And simplifying would make us greener.

It's the doing that is difficult.

Suspects Indeed

July 2008

BARRING THE UNFORESEEN, by the time this is posted we are ensconced in a house overlooking the Pacific Ocean near Yachats, Oregon.

It is the eighth edition of a biennial reunion that has been dubbed the Roundup of the Usual Suspects. Unlike that first gathering, we are approaching this iteration without trepidation.

The first roundup was almost happenstance. It brought together for the first time in decades four couples of us who had been close friends in our relative youth in St. Petersburg, Fla.

When we first became friends, we were all early in our careers and our married lives. We enjoyed being together, and our entertainment often consisted of having dinner at someone's house and watching the children play. We didn't have any pretensions, because we didn't have anything to be pretentious about.

Two of the couples left Florida in the early '70s. We all stayed in touch, swapping Christmas cards with the usual notes about the children and vacations. Some of us had seen each other now and then in the intervening years—a quick dinner on a business trip, that sort of thing—but those contacts had been fleeting. Even the two couples who remained in the St. Petersburg area lived far enough apart that they saw each other only occasionally.

The reunion idea was born when Tom and Jean, both of whom still lived in St. Petersburg, ran into each other. Tom mentioned completing what was to become his and Shirley's retirement home in the Rockies, and Jean said that would be a great place to get the old gang together.

And it happened. Everyone was interested enough, or curious enough, to work it into their schedules.

As we drove westward from Colorado Springs for that first gathering, I wondered whether we would still find common ground when we hadn't been together for more than 25 years. We were about to find out whether it was best to leave those glossy old memories unsmudged by current reality. Later, the others would admit having the same questions.

We should not have worried.

We were the last to arrive, and the others were gathered at the table eating chili. We slid into our seats and joined in.

Within minutes the intervening years had evaporated. I looked around the table. We all showed a little wear and tear, but we'd earned it. And in the important things, we were still the people we had been.

We weren't alike way back then, not by a long shot, but the things we shared in common were more than enough to let us accept the things that made us different, and we were comfortable with each other's shortcomings.

The reunion was enough to remind us that those early friendships are special treasures. It also was enough to tell us that we didn't want to wait 25 years for another get-together, so we decided to make it a biennial affair.

Since then we've met by the ocean in California, on Lake Martin in Alabama, in the mountains of Tennessee, at Lake Tahoe, on Mount Desert Island in Maine, and, two years ago, in St. Petersburg. We called that gathering the return to the scene of the crime.

All of us have hit a few bumps along the way, but on the whole we have been very lucky. We are still here, still married to the same spouses. We have raised our children and have been rewarded with grandchildren.

But, for a week or so, we will be in our 20s again. When we are together now, as it was then, we are all individual people, not someone's son or daughter, not someone's business associate or boss. We are important to each other because of who we are, not because of our title or economic standing.

And if our week together had a soundtrack, it would be filled with laugher.

That is a wonderful thing to keep.

Some Luck Involved

July 2008

I LOOK AT OUR two sons, grown now with children of their own, with wonder and some amazement—how did they turn out so, well, decent—and a small degree of pride—maybe we had something to do with it.

All of that is fresh in mind because the two of them were together with us for a couple of days over the July 4 holiday. That happens rarely—geography conspires to keep them apart—so I relished every moment, talking with them or just watching them enjoying each other.

Here were two people whom I respect and whose company I would enjoy even if they weren't kin to me.

As much as I would like to think that it was all our doing, I know that raising children doesn't work that way. There are no surefire rules for being a successful parent, though I am sure you could write down some surefire rules for being a failure.

A lot of us have had to learn parenting as we go along. I know I didn't have a real role model for being a dad. I never saw my father after my 16th summer and saw precious little of him before then.

We moved too often for me to have anyone who could be called a mentor.

Fortunately, most children are remarkably resilient, and I have come to believe that just being around counts for a lot.

I like to think that our sons learned some things from me. I know that I have learned a great deal from them and continue to do so.

From our older son, I have learned about optimism. He was born with the ability to see the positive side of almost any situation. You've got a flat tire? Aren't you lucky that you have a spare and that it isn't raining? That kind of mindset is not my nature, and I don't know how many times I have been taking a gloomy view only to think of what Jeff would say and have smiled.

From our younger son, I've grown to appreciate a longer perspective—and patience. Funny that he learned before I did that there are a lot of things that aren't nearly as important as we make them to be at the time, things we won't even remember. Just because other people have priorities that aren't the same as yours, it doesn't mean they're wrong

I watch our sons with their children, and I suspect that in many ways they are better fathers than I was. I only hope that they turn out to be as lucky as I have been.

Gone for Good

June 2009

IT HAS BEEN FOUR weeks since Hendry went missing, and I am gradually acknowledging that she is not coming back.

Still, every morning when I come downstairs, I look out the door to the side deck, half expecting her to be sitting there waiting for me to let her in and ready to give me a scolding for leaving her outside so long.

When I am dressing in the morning, I automatically reach out to the small step ladder I use for getting things down from the closet shelf as though she had hopped up to the top step and was waiting for me to scratch her ears.

When I sit down on the stair to put on my shoes, I expect her to come sit by my right side, always the right side, and to butt my hand with her head until I stop and give her the attention she craves.

Although Hendry technically is not our cat, we have been her people long enough for her to be a part of our daily lives. In theory, Hendry belongs to our son's family, but even as their cat, Hendry showed an independent streak that led our oldest granddaughter,

Nora, then eight years old, to proclaim, "Hendry belongs to the world."

It was Nora who gave Hendry her name. Her family adopted a small kitten when Nora was four. They thought it was a male, and they named it Henry. When Nora tried to say the name, though, it came out Hendry. So Hendry it became, and the name stuck, even after it turned out that Hendry was a she.

Our son's family lived next door to us in Montgomery then, and although Hendry spent a good deal of time outdoors, she never displayed any particular interest in us.

But a few weeks after our son's family moved several miles away, Hendry showed up at our house. Our son, who happened to be visiting us at the time, took Hendry home, and they kept her inside for several more weeks.

Hendry kept coming back, crossing several busy thoroughfares en route. So, even though we had decided not to have any more pets after Lightnin', our little Manx cat, disappeared, we took Hendry in, reasoning that sooner or later she was going to get hit by a car as she crossed one of those streets.

When we moved full time to the lake, we brought Hendry with us. We kept her inside for months, fearing she'd undertake a long trek back to her old neighborhood. She made no such effort; she was as content with the peace and quiet of the lake as we are.

Hendry craved attention only on her terms, and most of the time she was content simply to be in whatever room we were occupying. She would curl up on the couch in the living room, or sprawl on the floor in our bedroom as we slept. If we walked down to the dock, she followed along, although after having taken an unhappy ride on the pontoon boat she kept out of reach.

One of the times that she did demand attention was right after dinner. She seemed to sense when I had finished eating, and when I pushed away from the table, she would come sit by my chair until I made room for her to jump up beside me and have her ears scratched. When she'd had enough, she would jump down.

After Yellow Cat died, Hendry began spending more time outdoors, but she was mostly an indoor cat. She often wanted to go out in the evening. When we were ready to go upstairs at bedtime, I would go to the door. She was usually waiting to come in or sitting on the stoop or the railing contemplating the evening.

So when she was eager to go outside on a Wednesday evening, I opened the door and she scampered out. A couple of hours later we were ready to go up for the evening and I went to the door to let her in. She wasn't at the door or on the steps or on the railing. Nor was she on the hood of the car, another of her favorite perches.

She did not come when I called, which was not unusual. Dogs come when you call them; cats respond with studied indifference.

I expected that she would be waiting at the door the next morning, as she had been several times before, complaining loudly about being left out all night. But she was not there. We checked around the property; no sign of her or of a fight of any kind. The neighbors said they had not seen her. I checked along the roads near the house; no sign of a dead animal.

I had not wanted another pet, but with cats, you are chosen about as often as you choose.

But this time, like Sherman, if elected I will not serve.

Still, every morning when I come downstairs, the first thing I do is look to the door.

Perhaps She's Still Invisible

July 2009

THE REUNION OF THE Ruston (La.) High School Class of 1959 was, I imagine, very much like the 50th reunions of countless high school classes.

At the last reunion I attended, the 20th, the erosive qualities of time and gravity had begun to alter the landscape of our class, but now they had plowed deep furrows and dragged away our youth. I could have passed a lie detector test that I had never seen some of those people in my entire life.

(Memo to class reunion planners: Make the name tags really big, so people with failing eyesight aren't so obvious in trying to read a name as they squeeze a hand and say something like, "Hey, Robby, of course I remember you.")

I did not keep in touch with my classmates after I went away to college and essentially left my hometown for good. Many classmates remained in town or nearby, but over the years when I returned to visit, I spent most of the time with my brother and sister and with the diminishing number of other kinfolks.

The reunion events were limited: a tour of the old alma mater—

207

it has been renovated and expanded, but it was more recognizable than some of the alumni—and a party at the home of a class member.

In the weeks leading up to the reunion, it was natural to try to recall what school felt like at the time.

Racial segregation was still the order of the day, so our high school was all white. It was the only white high school, though, and as small as it was (about 110 in our class), it comprised a wide variety of people.

There were the kids who rode in from the country on big yellow buses. Many of the boys took classes in agriculture and shop and were distinguished by their blue corduroy Future Farmers of America jackets. Many of the girls took home ec and wore dresses that had been sewn by their mothers or had come from the bargain rack or a catalog. (There were exceptions, of course; no group is totally homogenous.)

There were the town kids—the children of business people and professors at the college in our town—who constituted the school's social elite.

There were, of course, the athletes who were a group in themselves and who had, at least for a time, acceptance by the elites.

The largest group was no group at all, that faceless middle that fell into that category simply because it did not fall into any other. I was one of those.

So, in some sense, the gathering of the Class of '59 was only partly a reunion, since for some the only union had been in being a member of that particular year's graduating class.

The high school years may be more difficult for girls than they are for boys. Our school, for example, had sororities, which by their very nature exclude people.

It started, I think, with one sorority—the upper tier as it were—followed by formation of another sorority, which I guess was composed of those who hadn't quite made the first cut. They were pretty exclusive themselves, so during my high school years, a group of girls who had not been invited to join either of the other groups formed their own club..

But some girls—and boys —were rejected by everyone, even that faceless middle.

There was a girl I remembered who always seemed as frightened as a cornered animal. She was obviously poor. Her clothes had the appearance of hand-me-downs, and I am not sure they were always clean. She did not seem to have any friends; I don't recall seeing her chatting with anyone in the halls or in the lunchroom. She never participated in class. I remember a time or two trying to start a conversation with her, but by then she must have been so wounded that she was suspicious of everyone.

I hadn't thought of her for at least 50 years, but she came to mind as I tried to recall those years. I wondered what had happened to her.

The reunion committee had done a good job of tracking down the members of the Class of '59, and they handed out a sheet with the names and addresses of the living and a list of the departed.

On the entire list there were only two names that had no information at all. Hers was one of them. No one knew her then; no one knew her now.

Not Charlie

December 2009

WHEN EACH BIENNIAL Roundup of the Usual Suspects is winding down, we agree on a location for the next reunion, and someone takes responsibility for scouting out locations and making arrangements.

In our minds, we Usual Suspects are still the four young couples that we were in the mid-1960s when our friendships formed in St. Petersburg, Fla. Photos from the '60s, from our first reunion in 1994, and the most recent one last year, however, would reveal the irresistible tug of time.

It has been a long journey.

Just getting accustomed to being adults and too poor to be pretentious, we were friends simply because we liked each other. We are friends now because we still like each other.

We could have missed knowing that, though, except for a lunchtime conversation.

Jean and Charlie had remained in St. Petersburg, and Tom and Shirley lived in Clearwater. The two couples did not see each other often, but Jean and Tom both worked in downtown St. Petersburg and often lunched in the same place.

By then Chuck and Leanne and Adelaide and I had long been gone from St Petersburg. They were settled in Claremont, Calif., and we lived in Montgomery, Ala.

One day at lunch, Jean suggested that the four couples have a reunion at the house Tom and Shirley had built in the mountains of Colorado in anticipation of retirement.

I think curiosity impelled all of us to attend that first reunion, and we approached it with questions and a certain amount of trepidation. Within minutes of the last couple's arrival, the intervening years were swept away, and the Usual Suspects were born.

We agreed that meeting every other year would keep the reunions from becoming a duty, and the schedule gave us something to look forward to. The primary site specification was that there be room for all of us to hang out.

If you listened to a sound track of our gatherings, you would understand why. You would hear laughter, punctuated by barbs that would make you wonder how the verbal combatants could possibly be friends. We are armed with sharp tongues, but we never draw blood.

Each time a Roundup of the Usual Suspects ends, we know that our numbers might be diminished before the next gathering. Mortality is a reality, and as the years pass, the horizon comes closer.

Still, in the summer of 2008 when our reunion on the Oregon coast broke up, none of us expected that the first person missing would be Charlie.

Charlie was full of life, passionate and curious and energetic. He loved corny jokes and bad puns, and he would tell them with relish, knowing that his reward would be a chorus of groans.

He loved his native St. Petersburg and the starkly beautiful Four Corners of the Southwest and the brooding mountains of

Tennessee. And because he loved them, he acquired a depth of knowledge about the flora and the fauna and the people of each region.

He loved visiting rock shops, and he polished stones to decorate the exquisite wooden boxes that he crafted.

He and Jean were the perfect pair. And he was positively gaga about his grandchildren.

In all the years, we had never known Charlie to be ill with anything.

But not long after he and Jean returned home from the reunion, Charlie was diagnosed with lymphoma. Chemotherapy drove it away, and last spring Jean and Charlie and Adelaide and I spent a week in his beloved mountains celebrating his remission from lymphoma and my recovery from bypass surgery.

The lymphoma had retreated, but it had not surrendered, and it returned last summer more virulent than before.

Charlie died just before Christmas.

So early in January six of the Usual Suspects will go to St. Petersburg. We will join Jean at a memorial service for her husband and our friend.

Adelaide and I will share our son's observation upon learning of Charlie's death: "To make a difference and to be well remembered is something everyone aspires to."

Certainly Charlie achieved that and much more.

But knowing that does not ease the sting of his departure.

Cost of Complacency

May 2010

THE FOLLOWING WAS written Sunday, but I could not post it for
lack of an internet connection: I am writing this with one hand
while sitting in a room in UAB Hospital in Birmingham. The other
hand, swathed in bandages, is being held vertically higher than my
heart to keep fluids from building up in the thumb doctors sewed
back on Friday night.

It was a near thing. The surgery resident who was attending me
had consulted with his boss and was already numbing the area
around my dangling left thumb, preparing to amputate right there
in the emergency room, His pager summoned him. His boss
apparently had taken another look at the X-rays and decided it
might be possible to save the thumb. I don't know whether he knew
that I am left handed.

The upshot was that a surgical team spent four or five hours
putting back together nerves and blood vessels, and I am tethered to
an IV pole that is infusing me with antibiotics and blood thinner to
try to prevent the vessels and capillaries from getting plugged up.

The surgeon stopped by earlier this afternoon and said things are looking pretty good, though nothing is certain. He explained that he could not save the nail bed and that he pulled a flap of skin up to cover the missing nail. If it works, the thumb will be a little shorter with the first joint fused.If the flap fails, the thumb will be shorter still.

As so often is the case, there was no indication that disaster was looming,

On Friday morning, I was working alone in my neighbor's shop on some Adirondack chairs for our front deck. I have worked with tools and wood almost all of my life. I know the safety rules, and like many others, I have skirted the safety rules from time to time without suffering consequences.

Until Friday. A moving saw blade, a hand too near it, and a mangled thumb. No one was around, so I wrapped my T-shirt around my hand and walked home. My wife was not at home and I couldn't reach her on her cell phone, so I found some gauze and tape and wrapped my hand and drove to Alexander City to the Russell Medical Center emergency room. They quickly determined that I needed to go to UAB and made arrangements.

I had plenty of time during the ambulance ride to reflect on my own folly, and I am no less chagrined by hearing the doctors' stories about power tool accidents much more catastrophic than mine. I've had time to consider, too, that it is not just guys with tools who grow dangerously complacent after years of getting by.

Recent reports about inattention in airline cockpits have stirred concern.

And I suspect that the many of the people aboard that oil-drilling rig in the Gulf of Mexico were doing things they've done for years.

The consequences of my complacency were great enough. Complacency on a larger scale can be truly catastrophic.

Back to the Shop

June 2010

MY BROTHER, MY SISTER and I concluded not long ago that our real hobbies are work.

So it is with some difficulty that I am spending a great deal of time sitting around with my left hand elevated to try to reduce the swelling in my mangled-but-repaired left thumb. (I should note here that we are fortunate to have an institution like UAB Hospital so near, and I was even more fortunate that Dr. Ian Marrero was available. I am told he is the person you want to fix your hand, and I will endorse that statement.)

I was fretting the other day about all of the things I need/want to do, but I reminded myself, "Well, dimwit, if you hadn't stuck your thumb in the table saw, you wouldn't be having to work on the patience thing."

The reactions I get from acquaintances have been interesting. Sympathy, of course. Some people recall their own close calls— anyone who has spent any time working with power tools has had a close call—or talk about someone they know who did. Some people ask whether I plan to stay away from power tools. I tell them I think I'll just call Blue Cross and tell them I'm planning to make some more Adirondack chairs and they will say, "Hey, we'll bring you some. What color do you want?"

It's funny. A friend of mine had a moment of inattention not long ago and crashed his car. I'll bet no one will ask him whether he plans to stop driving.

Of course I will go back to the shop—just as quickly as I am able. A saw is no more dangerous than an automobile. Both will let you get away with being careless, until they don't. I will just look at what's left of my thumb and use it as a reminder to pay more attention to the things that can hurt you.

Tiny Knot, Great Progress

August 2010

LETTER TO A friend in Minnesota:

Today marked a significant milestone on the road from my near self-amputation.

I managed to tie a small fly onto a tiny tippet. Never mind that it took 15 minutes to do it. Never mind that the fish were not the least bit interested in what I was offering them. I, by George, tied a tiny improved clinch knot.

My left thumb still has not fully healed. The plastic surgeon will decide early next month whether he needs to graft some skin onto a small spot that has stubbornly refused to heal thus far. But my only bandage is a large Band-Aid, and although my fingers are stiff from having been in a splint and the part of my thumb that still moves is equally restricted, after four long months I am beginning to think I may be able to resume being a left hander.

I managed to put my left hand in my pocket the other day, something I had not done since May 21, and I am able to hold a pen in my left hand and move it to produce something that looks pretty much like my handwriting. I did manage to write my name with the right hand. It had a cramped look, like the signature of someone who has learned to write his name but who really can't read and write. When I had to write some checks on an account that I am the only signatory to, I stopped by the bank to make sure the checks wouldn't be rejected as forgeries. My friend at the bank put a note on my account that if anyone had a question about my checks they should consult with him. Another reason for loving a small town.

The temporary incapacity does have some advantages, as my older son, who always sees the glass half full, would be quick to recognize. I can eat right-handed, a skill that can come in handy at a crowded table We lefties always look for a corner seat to avoid the battle of the elbows; now I can sit at the middle of the table if need be.

I have gone the whole summer without getting my left hand wet. I fished (spinning rod) several times with Griffin, the older grandson, who was here for nearly two months, but I couldn't paddle, so we settled for fishing from the dock. I'm counting on it being healed by November, when I'm supposed to go paddling in the Okefenokee with some friends. If it doesn't, I guess I'll just tie a bag around my hand.

And, at long last, I can type with both hands. I haven't written much of anything for the past four months because I was reduced to typing with my right hand. Now I'm typing with nine fingers.

There is, of course, a lot that I still can't do—I'm eager to get started on some rehab to help take care of some of that—but, by golly, I got that fly tied to the tippet this morning, and that was enough to make me feel like I'm going in the right direction.

Hope your summer is going well.

Just Call Me ... Bob?

February 2011

MY PARENTS SADDLED me with the given name of William, which naturally evolved into Bill. I was named after my father, whose name was David Herbert, but who for some reason had acquired the nickname Bill.

There's nothing intrinsically wrong with the name Bill. It's just that the name Bill Brown is so common that even the smallest burg has two or three. And not all of them are people whom you wish to be confused with. Every time we've ever purchased a house, I have had to sign affidavits that I am not the Bill Brown who has had a mortgage foreclosed, filed bankruptcy, or has some other blot on his record.

When your last name is Brown, you definitely need a given name—or nickname—that has more than one syllable.

From childhood to high school graduation, people called me Billy; some people in my hometown still call me Billy. But when I got to college, everyone automatically called me Bill—it sounded more grownup, I think—and it has been Bill ever since.

Except that it hasn't been, and I can't exactly blame my parents, though I think having a first and last name start with the same letter is at least a contributing factor.

It didn't begin until after I graduated from college, but since then, an amazing number of people get fixed into their minds that my name is Bob.

It is not just strangers to whom I am introduced as Bill and who two minutes later are calling me Bob. As a young reporter, I covered City Hall in St. Petersburg, Fla. On my news gathering rounds, I stopped in the city manager's office every day. About half of the time the receptionist greeted me as Bob. I would correct her, and I would be Bill for a day or two, but then I would revert to Bob. Her explanation for the name confusion was, "You just look like a Bob."

I suppose Shakespeare—or Juliet (What's in a name? that which we call a rose / By any other name would smell as sweet)—was right, but still I used to bridle at being called Bob. No longer, though. People whom I see regularly, including one whose own nickname is Bill, alternate between calling me Bill and Bob. I just smile and respond to whatever name they call me; I guess if I ever run for office, I will have to put my name on the ballot as Bill Bob Brown.

(My wife, whose given name is Adelaide, has a totally different problem. No one calls her Shirley or Barbara or Sue. But they can't seem to say Adelaide. It comes out Adeline, Adalie, and even Natalie. Like me, she's learned to put up with it.)

Still, I wonder what a Bob looks like.

Youth Exits in a Garbage Bag

January 2010

FROM THE DARK recesses of the attic, I retrieved a couple of file storage boxes labeled "Bill's Stuff" to search for some tax records.

I didn't find the tax records; it turned out that I didn't need them anyway.

What I did find was fragments of my long ago youth, clippings that marked a career in newspapers that began in 1962.

"By William Brown" the bylines read, although no one called me William. The St. Petersburg Times of that day insisted on using given names in bylines; there were no Bills or Bobs or Chucks. (Male Times reporters also wore ties and jackets when many of the other media representatives were wearing sport shirts.)

The clippings were folded and brittle, but as I browsed through them, they took on color and smell and shape. I could remember what things looked like and smelled like and even tasted like (blue sky that went on forever and thunderheads that seemed to portend the end of the world, the soft smell of tropical flowers and the tang of salt air, smoked mullet at Ted Peters and black beans and rice and crusty Cuban bread at the Jockey Club).

221

For a little while I was a newly minted college graduate setting out on a great adventure. There was my first byline only a few days after I'd started work on a story about a fatal traffic accident at Roosevelt Boulevard and Ninth Street North. I could recall following the police officers and the gurney down the hallway in the emergency room at Mound Park Hospital and watching one of the doctors pull the sheet over the victim's head.

Welcome to the real world.

The clippings in the stack were eclectic:

Murders and suicides and fires and accidents.

Feuding politicians and ambitious land developers.

A story about the great freeze of 1962, written on an old Smith-Corona portable typewriter by the light of a fire in an orange grove in Pasco County as the growers fought, mostly unsuccessfully, to keep their crop from freezing.

An interview with the creator of the long-running soap opera "The Edge of Night" who mailed in his scripts from his home in Sarasota.

A thoroughbred horse auction in Ocala.

There were columns, too, complete with a photo of a kid who must have been me.

It is perhaps vanity, but even the routine stories still read well.

The clippings ended when I became an editor and didn't appear again until years later when I began writing a column regularly.

I looked at that pile of clippings and thought: What a grand and glorious adventure it truly was.

But it was my adventure. To anyone else they would just be a pile of old newsprint.

So I picked out a few of them to help stoke the fires of memory. The rest of my long ago youth I put in a black plastic bag and took out to the garbage can.